Making S

Due

MW00978777

Contents

For Lynne

PREFACE

This book was written with two types of people in mind. First, I've written a book for Christians who would like to know more about *what* they believe and *why*. The desired result is that they will be able to describe and defend their faith with a greater sense of confidence.

Second, I've written a book for non-Christians who may want more information about what Christians believe. They may even wonder if personal faith is a valid option in today's world of technological "certainty." Hopefully they will find that the Christian faith not only makes sense, but it is a compelling explanation of life and the world.

Deciding what goes into a book like this is only slightly less difficult than deciding what must be left out. I have chosen to focus on matters of faith which affect the fundamental points of Christianity as they conflict with a non-Christian worldview. For this reason, many debatable issues which are current among Christians have been omitted. There are many books available which discuss these issues at length.

If you are like me, you enjoy clever quotes, analogies, and stories which illustrate principles. I have included many of these throughout the book in the hope that they will clarify truths which sometimes get lost in abstract arguments.

I believe strongly that if Christians have a vision to love God with their minds as well as their hearts, an appealing and resilient faith will be the result.

May God bless this work in your life.

Acknowledgments

I would like to express my heartfelt appreciation to

... Joe and DeLo Brown, my parents, who taught me about faith through their lives;

... Anna Smith, my secretary, who gave a great deal of her time to type and correct the manuscript;

... my dear colleague, Dr. W. Gary Phillips, who read several of the chapters and gave helpful (and funny) suggestions;

... the good people at VICTOR BOOKS, particularly Mr. James Adair, Mr. Mark Sweeney, and Mrs. Afton Rorvik, for their encouragement and guidance;

... Lynne, my wife, for her constant love and understanding;

... April, my daughter, for not writing on the final copy.

INTRODUCTION: *Why Believe?*

Faith is to believe, on the Word of God, what we do not see, and its reward is to see and enjoy what we believe.
St. Augustine

Now faith is the assurance of things hoped for, the conviction of things not seen.
Hebrews 11:1

"Why do you believe in God?" She lit a cigarette and leaned back against the wall. Here in Eastern Europe, she rarely had an opportunity to discuss religious views with someone who believed. Most of her fellow countrymen did not trust her because of her government connections. She had described herself to me as "Marxist to the core." Her mother was a leading member of the Communist Party in the country; her father a police superintendent.

"God has made Himself known in what He has made," I responded and gave her a short survey of the classical arguments for the existence of God.

She seemed not to hear. "Is God sovereign over history?"

"Sure," I replied. "God is totally in control."

"Then explain to me why He orchestrated the Holocaust. Millions of people brutally and senselessly murdered by Hitler. What kind of sovereign God plays such games with His creation?"

Before I could think of an answer, my Communist friend rehearsed the atrocities and wars committed in the name of religion—events in modern Ireland and the Middle East, the Inquisition, the Puritan oppression, and the debauchery of the organized church in the Middle Ages. Her knowledge of religion and the history of its failings overwhelmed me.

When I failed to respond, she put out her cigarette and looked me straight in the face. Her eyes were pleading. "Tell me," she asked softly. "Why do you believe?"

I cannot remember what I said, but I know I felt inadequate and outmatched. I had a hard time making sense of my faith in the face of someone who had serious questions.

Her question haunted me: "Why do you believe?" With my background in mathematics and science, I didn't usually believe easily in anything. Yet I had never asked myself, "Why do I believe?" I realized that I needed to understand my own faith before I could explain it to others.

Faith is an inescapable part of being a Christian. Christians are called "believers" or "those who believe," and faith is such a crucial theme in Scripture that words describing it occur over 500 times in the New Testament alone.

But faith has fallen on hard times. The vibrant, life-changing, life-controlling faith of the New Testament appears shrouded behind a heavy mist of doubt and uncertainty. Even among Christians, faith may be shoved aside and become only a peripheral part of life, rather than a central, motivating force. Why has this happened? The answer is found on two levels.

First, on the practical level it is easy for us to rely on human institutions and relationships to take care of our needs. Like the little boy who grew tired of praying to a God he couldn't see and wanted "to talk to somebody with skin on," we desire tangible assurances that our basic needs will be supplied. Thus, we have not felt a need to trust in God.

While my parents were visiting Sweden several years ago, they took a guided tour through the historic churches of Stockholm. The guide matter-of-factly noted that although 95 percent of the people belong to the church, only 5 percent actually attend services.

"Why?" my father asked. The tour guide shrugged. "Who needs God when the government gives you everything?"

In the Western world, we have an insane attachment to things, with the result that any need for God is secondary to an increased income, financial security, the next vacation, or a new car. Why believe when everything we need and want is so readily at our disposal?

Second, on a much deeper level, believing in the "unseen things of God" is no longer fashionable in an age that craves the certainty of technology. Having lost a sense of the transcendent, we may sing "This Is My Father's World," yet in the back of our minds we seek scientific explanations for everything that happens.

God cannot be observed, we are told, so belief in God's existence is an unscientific belief. Our reasons for believing seem to pale before the vast storehouse of facts that technology spews forth, and we may wonder if science has made believing obsolete.

So here we stand, unsure why we believe yet somehow convinced that we should. The Bible tells us clearly that "without faith it is impossible to please God" (Heb. 11:6), so we maintain our faith, not wishing to bring down divine displeasure on ourselves.

In the first part of this book, we will look at the relationship between faith and science to determine if irreconcilable differences really do exist. What is science? What is faith? By understanding scientific inquiry and then exploring what it means to believe, we will see that the two are partners rather than enemies. The Christian need not be ashamed or even hesitant to boldly announce, "Yes, I believe!" Believing is natural, powerful, and necessary.

Once we understand what it means to believe, we must focus on the actual content of our belief.

What we believe is the key element of faith. True faith in God involves believing truth about Him; therefore, the second part of this book will be devoted to the importance of right belief and the consequences and dangers of believing error. We will discuss why we should believe in God, Jesus Christ, the Bible, and the hope of eternity. These beliefs lay the foundation on which the Christian life is to be lived.

Each chapter concludes with a number of questions for review and application. A list of books under the heading "Further Reading" is also included at the end of each chapter. These lists are for those who would like to explore the subject matter further or recommend books to friends.

PART ONE: THE BASICS OF BELIEVING

CHAPTER ONE
What Does It Mean to Believe?

Faith is believing what you know ain't so.
A schoolboy quote by Mark Twain

Faith—is the Pierless Bridge
Supporting what we see
Unto the scene that we do not—
Too slender for the eye
Emily Dickinson

Faith of the Everyday Kind

Mason didn't like talking about religion. He had already spent enough time in prison to see other inmates "get saved" in the hope of obtaining an early parole for good behavior. Being active in the religious functions in the prison went on an inmate's record, so it was a good thing to do.

But Mason wasn't going to play the game. When I talked with him about his relationship to the Lord, he shook his head. "Naw, I don't believe in anything."

Of course, Mason does believe in many things—we all do—he just does not believe in God.

Belief is a common element in every part of our lives. Most of the truths we hold as certain are ones we have accepted with some degree of faith. We may call it "trusting" or "having confidence in" or "reliance," but they are all forms of the act of believing.

For example, in school my history teacher described the various events of the American Revolution, and I believed her. Now, there is no way that I could have possibly verified the many facts she related to me. If I had been so inclined, I might have gone to the library and researched the Revolution in encyclopedias and history books in order to insure that what she said happened actually occurred. But I still would not have escaped the necessity of faith; I merely would have shifted my trust to the writers of the books I read, even though they themselves saw none of the events they described. In fact, they were believing the writings and testimonies of others.

Much of our education is based squarely on this type of faith. We usually accept and believe what we are taught. Whether the subject is psychology, business, history, or English, we feel disposed to trust the one presenting the material to us.

Beyond formal education, our lives are filled with repeated acts of faith. We pick up the morning newspaper and believe that a fire in Brandon, Florida destroyed nine buildings, that the Cowboys beat the Redskins, or that it rained in Indianapolis. We usually accept these reports with unwavering faith, never feeling the necessity to confirm their occurrence.

Every day we put our trust in a number of things or a variety of people, including package labeling (is this *really* aspirin?) and car manufacturers (will my brakes *really* stop the car?). Sometimes our faith in these areas leads to tragedy, like people dying after taking cyanide-laced capsules. The crime itself was easily perpetrated because of the public's general trust that medicine purchased in stores contains exactly what the outside label describes.

Suppose that we decide only to accept truths that we have personally observed or experienced. How much would we "know"? We would soon realize that we unquestionably affirm as truth very little that we have not accepted by faith. Trust—committing oneself to truths without the benefit of "scientific" confirmation—is faith in its most basic form.

Examples of everyday faith point to the fact that we are creatures who have both the inclination and the desire to believe. It is not absurd to believe; it is most natural and necessary.

Faith That Answers the Ultimate Questions

Everyday faith is a long way from faith in God. There is a big difference between believing in God and believing that Washington crossed the Delaware. Faith in God answers the ultimate questions of life and is intensely personal.

Many questions about ourselves and our universe pester us for an answer. Before he became a Christian, Russian novelist Leo Tolstoy listed six crucial questions that he had to answer.

1. Why am I living?
2. What is the cause of my existence and that of everything else?
3. Why do I exist?
4. Why is there a division of good and evil within me?
5. How must I live?
6. What is death—how can I save myself?[1]

These are among the ultimate questions of life that science cannot answer. The agnostic has taken the position that the answers to these questions are unknowable *(a=no; gnostic=knowledge)*. But he is only fooling himself by thinking he can avoid such issues. We cannot escape coming to conclusions about our purpose and destiny and the existence of God.

Though not outwardly religious in the usual sense of the word, many people have answered the ultimate questions of life in one way or another.

They may reject God and choose to "believe in" human potential or something else. They may answer the ultimate questions of life by calling their existence a chance occurrence with no purpose or plan. But faith in God provides specific, comforting answers to these questions. Blind chance is replaced by God's personal plan for all He has made.

Faith in God is also intensely personal. By this I mean that faith is more than an intellectual exercise, an acknowledgment that certain facts are true. Rather, faith in God involves the commitment of the whole person to another Person. The ultimate questions of man's existence are not explained by impersonal forces or mathematical equations but by a personal God with whom we can relate by faith.

Faith: The Center of Life

James was at the top of his field. As a real estate developer, his vast land holdings and projects made him one of the wealthiest and most recognizable men in the state. Being an active Christian, James used his wealth and influence for the Lord in many ways. Anyone in need who came to his attention received help. He made many opportunities to share Christ with politicians and corporate presidents. He had a reputation for being upbeat and fun-loving.

Then the real estate crunch hit and James' small financial empire began to crumble. He struggled for months, valiantly trying to protect his investments and development projects. It was a losing battle; his empire collapsed.

Many of his colleagues panicked or were thrown into depression. Some committed suicide. But James continued as before, smiling, laughing, and always active in the Lord's work.

"You lost everything," a friend reminded him. "How can you be so happy?"

James smiled. "As long as I have the Lord, I have everything."

After hearing James' testimony, a prison inmate said, "I get tired of hearing rich people talk about how God is blessing them. It's something else to hear how someone has lost millions—and God is still blessing him. That's faith!"

James found himself in a situation much like that of the biblical character Job, who lost most of his worldly possessions and was forced to confront the quality of his faith. Like Job, James maintained a trust in God that went beyond his bank account. He often quoted the words of Job: "Naked I came from my mother's womb, and naked I shall return there. The Lord gave and the Lord has taken away Blessed be the name of the Lord" (Job 1:21).

For James, faith was much more than an intellectual assent to certain truths. Faith was life. His security was not in things but in the immovable Lord, and his faith gave his life a stability that could not be shaken.

This is the faith described in the Bible. For the Old Testament saint, to believe meant to trust, hope, fear, and obey. Faith in God was grounded in His unchanging character and looked backward at what God had done in the past as assurance that He would continue faithfully in His relationship to His people.

Expressing faith in God was a bold declaration on the part of the believer. A key Old Testament word for faith is the Hebrew *aman* from which we get our "Amen." To believe in God was literally to say "Amen" to God.

The heart of the concept of faith in the Old Testament is the quality of "reliability" or "steadfastness." In an uncertain and wavering world, the believer laid hold of what he perceived as steadfast in the hope of becoming steadfast himself.

Imagine clinging to a rock in the turbulent white water of a fast-moving river. Laying hold of the immovable rock keeps you from being swept away by the violent flow. In the Old Testament, faith is pictured as providing a similar type of stability.

Many Old Testament saints placed their faith in God, asking Him to preserve them from an opposing army or the ravages of a drought. The Lord was seen as steadfast in the midst of an overwhelming flood of adversity

The close connection between faith and security is evident in the life of King Ahaz. Isaiah 7 describes the attempts of Ahaz to defend himself against the advancing armies of the Syrian-Israeli coalition. His attempts to find security in an alliance with Assyria are rebuked by Isaiah, who admonishes the king to turn to God for protection: "If you will not believe, you surely shall not last [i.e., be established]" (Isa. 7:9). The same word is used for "believe" and "last." By laying hold of the steadfast God, the King himself would be secure both in his life and in his position.

The Three Elements of Faith

Clearly, faith is not a static concept in the Bible, and the terminology employed to describe it does not always have the same emphasis. Sometimes faith is described as the accepting of a certain statement as true. For example, Jesus asked the Jews, "If I speak truth, why do you not believe Me?" (John 8:46)

Other times, faith is explained as the response at a crisis event, such as the moment of salvation or healing (i.e., Acts 16:31; Matt. 9:22). Still more often, faith is described as an attitude of trusting; a commitment of oneself to God that can be tested (James 1:3), increased (2 Thes. 1:3), and perfected (James 2:22).

These different descriptions of faith do not suggest different types of faith but rather different levels of submission to what is believed. To understand what it means to have faith, let's look at these three aspects of faith: assent, trust, and commitment.

Assent

Assent is the most basic component of faith. It involves accepting propositional statements as truth. Theologians often describe this as "believe-that" type of faith: "I believe *that* God exists"; "I believe *that* Jesus died on the cross"; etc. The emphasis is on the *content* of what is being believed.

Why Do We Believe? What pushes us to accept propositional statements as truth? What causes us to believe that God exists? One cause is *tradition.* How many people do you know who believe in God because their parents did? Atheism, agnosticism, and most of the other "isms" can be passed on in the same way. Many believe certain truths simply because they have always believed them.

Tradition is not a wrong reason for holding to particular beliefs. The Bible confirms the method of parents passing on their belief in God and adherence to the Law as an essential part of child-rearing (Deut. 6:4-9). But passing on wrong beliefs in the family is just as possible, so there is no guarantee that traditional faith is accurate.

Another factor which pushes us to believe that God exists is *reason.* A person may be convinced by good, sound arguments that something is true. This is what happened when Paul confounded the Jews in Damascus by "proving that this Jesus is the Christ" (Acts 9:22). We can almost hear Paul explaining how Jesus fulfilled the Old Testament prophecies of the Messiah, answering every question and objection, so that many of the Jews were convinced by the sheer logic of his arguments.

A third factor causing us to believe is *the work of the Holy Spirit.* The Spirit came into the world to "convict the world concerning sin, righteousness, and judgment" (John 16:8). This convincing is an internal and spiritual work whereby we are made aware of our own moral shortcomings and the certainty of judgment. How shall we escape? Answering this question is the first step in the quest for peace within, often causing us to recognize the "God-shaped vacuum" in our hearts.

The Limits of Assent. We may ask, what good is purely intellectual assent? The answer is obvious: it is the starting point, the place where all further commitments begin.

The importance of this aspect of faith cannot be overlooked. The Apostle Paul ties salvation to the person who believes *that* Jesus died and rose from the dead (Rom. 10:9; 1 Thes. 4:14). The Apostle John declares that the events and teachings recorded in his Gospel were intended to move his readers to believe *that* Jesus is the Christ, the Son of God (John 20:31). All belief has some factual content. *What* we believe is important, and we will discuss this in the next chapter. But is believing the *right facts* enough?

James clearly addresses this question when he writes, "You believe that God is one. You do well; the demons also believe, and shudder. But are you willing to recognize, you foolish fellow, that faith without works is useless?" (James 2:19-20)

Notice that James never denies that the individuals in question have faith; but he questions the usefulness of purely intellectual faith. "You believe God is one; big deal," he seems to be saying. "So do the demons. In fact, they *know* there is one God because they have seen Him."

Purely intellectual assent to truth is certainly the starting point of faith, but it is not the end.

Trust

A second biblical aspect of faith is the concept of *trust.* Whereas assent is the intellectual acceptance of a truth, trust is more of an emotional reliance on a person. For example, I may intellectually assent to the fact that my doctor knows exactly what he is doing. I can give reasons for my belief by citing his education and experience. I believe that he can take care of my medical needs, and I even express my confidence to him and others. But when he informs me that he must operate on me, my intellectual assent must blossom into personal trust before I allow him to excavate my body.

There is an obvious difference between *believing* in God and *trusting* in God. Trust is faith moving out of the mental realm and involving the whole person. Trust, of course, is built on assent because I cannot trust God unless I first believe that He exists. The writer of Hebrews states, "And without faith it is impossible to please Him; for he who comes to God must believe that He is, and that He is a rewarder of those who seek Him" (Heb. 11:6). The believer's trust in God's goodness (as a "rewarder") comes after he first acknowledges God's existence.

Trust in God involves at least three different characteristics. First, trust is directed toward God as a Person. Trust does not seek facts *about* God but rather seeks a relationship *with* God. As Paul noted, "I know whom I have believed" (2 Tim. 1:12). His faith led him to an intimate knowledge of a Person ("whom"), not a set of facts.

Pascal once said, "The knowledge of God is very far from the love of God."[2] Every trusting relationship involves an emotional commitment. Notice David's trust and confidence in the personal God: "But as for me, I trust in Thee, O Lord, I say 'Thou art my God.' My times are in Thy hand" (Ps. 31:14-15).

Second, trust is a reliance on someone else in matters beyond our control. When we put ourselves in the hands of experts such as doctors, lawyers, or taxi drivers, we are exercising trust. They are "authorities" in their areas of expertise. We rely on them because they supposedly know more about our situation than we do and thus are in a better position to take care of us.

God has infinite knowledge and power. The ultimate questions of life are no mystery to Him because He alone created the universe and is carrying out His plans and purposes. Acknowledging His expertise, we entrust our lives and our future destiny to the hands of God. Isaiah speaks of this trust as a song that Judah shall sing: "The steadfast of mind Thou wilt keep in perfect peace, because he trusts in Thee. Trust in the Lord forever, for in God the Lord, we have an everlasting Rock" (Isa. 26:3-4).

Finally, trust is rooted in the faithful character of God. He is consistent, just, and kind (Ps. 136:1; Mal. 3:6). He always has our best in mind and deals with us accordingly. If God were capricious and vacillating, we would have no basis for trusting Him. But God is "trustworthy," worthy of our complete trust.

Some question the goodness of God: if God is all-good and all-powerful, why is there undeserved suffering in the world? We will discuss this more in chapter 4, but here we must point out that evil in the world is the result of man's rebellion against God and not a reflection of God's character. The Bible views suffering as an intrusion into the world which God created totally good (Gen. 1–3). However we try to understand the evil present today, we must never forget that God's Son experienced suffering that was completely undeserved. It is only because of God's unchanging goodness that the promise of universal justice and the destruction of evil (Rev. 21:1-4) has any meaning.

Commitment

An outgrowth of assent and trust is commitment; that is, faith manifested in the way we live. How does what I believe affect my lifestyle, the decisions I make, the way I spend my time and money?

Most preaching is directed to this aspect of faith. We all try to practice the truths that we believe, but all too often what is so dear to us in our minds and hearts is not reflected in our actions. Then we ask ourselves, do we really believe?

Commitment can be measured at different levels: *acceptance* (when we are willing to be identified with what we believe); *preference* (when we actively seek to know more about what we believe); and *full commitment* (when we guide our public lives by what we believe and are constrained to share our faith with others).[3]

A person may desire to identify himself with Christianity and thus begin attending a local church. He is operating at the level of *acceptance*—he publicly associates himself with what he says he believes. Suppose he becomes interested in learning more about his faith, so he begins to study the Bible and books on Christianity. He is expressing his commitment at the level of *preference* by investing time and effort to grow in his faith. *Full commitment* comes when his faith develops into the guiding principle of his behavior, and he begins to share what he believes with others.

Philosophers and theologians debate whether a person can truly "believe" one thing but live a lifestyle contrary to that belief. Is a person only deceiving himself mentally while actually portraying his true faith by the way he lives?

Let's go back to my doctor. If I tell everyone what a wonderful doctor he is and how I trust him with my life, then most of those around me would be convinced that I had great faith in him. But if, when he informs me of my need for an operation, I begin to tremble with fear, and I begin to doubt his diagnosis, then my "great faith" will be questioned. Furthermore, if I chose to ignore his advice and still continue to tell everyone how much I trust him, what sort of faith will I be demonstrating? Most people will conclude that I am deceiving myself (and others) about my faith in the doctor.

It is not difficult to see how this same lack of commitment in faith can apply to our faith in God. Of course, self-deception is a reality for many people. They think they are doing everything right, only to discover that God disagrees. James speaks of the deception of being a hearer of God's Word but not a doer, and of the religious person who cannot control his tongue (James 1:22, 26).

Faith that only hears is not acceptable faith in the biblical sense. We may intellectually acknowledge and profess our faith in God, but it is our lives that demonstrate our true nature: "They profess to know God, but by their deeds they deny Him" (Titus 1:16).

Commitment, as an aspect of faith, is a continual outworking of what we believe and trust in our hearts. As our belief and trust in God increase, so does our commitment to a lifestyle of faith. Often our commitment to God grows most rapidly when tested by circumstances or temptations.

Abraham's faith was publicly vindicated when he offered up his son Isaac (Gen. 22:1-19). But more important, his faith was "perfected," or matured, as a result of this life-and-death situation (James 2:21-23). His trust in God went so far as to believe that God would raise Isaac from the dead, even though such a resurrection had never occurred before (Heb. 11:17-19). Abraham's unswerving commitment to God grew out of his intellectual belief and personal trust in God.

The Fullness of Faith

Assent, trust, and commitment: these three words explain the fullness of faith. Faith involves the whole person, including the mind, the heart, and the will.

But in all of this discussion of faith, we cannot forget the work of the Holy Spirit who brings us to God as a new creation, guiding our journey through faith. Salvation becomes a reality as God's grace works through our belief, trust, and commitment toward Him (Eph. 2:8-9).

Now, we must ask the question: Is faith relevant in today's world? After all, we live in an age of complicated technology and computer-generated thinking. Hasn't science eliminated the need for faith? We will discuss these issues in the next chapter as we explore the relationship between faith and science.

Discussion Questions

1. Give some examples of how you have expressed the "everyday" type of faith today.

2. How does religious faith differ from the everyday type of faith?

3. Why does the word "faith" occur so infrequently in the Old Testament?

4. Describe the distinctive differences among the three aspects of faith: assent, trust, and commitment. Give a practical example of each.

5. Which of the three aspects of faith is being emphasized in the following verses:
   John 1:12-13?
   Ephesians 2:8-9?
   Romans 3:21-22?
   Hebrews 11:1?
   James 1:2-3?

6. Discuss the source of some of your beliefs. Do you believe what you do because of tradition, reason, or the work of the Holy Spirit?

Further Reading

David Cook, *Thinking About Faith* (Grand Rapids: Zondervan Publishing House, 1986).

C. Stephen Evans, *The Quest for Faith* (Downers Grove, Ill.: InterVarsity Press, 1982).

David Wolfe, *Epistemology: The Justification of Belief* (Downers Grove, Ill.: InterVarsity Press, 1982).

Nicholas Wolterstorff, *Reason Within the Bounds of Religion*, 2nd edition (Grand Rapids: Eerdmans, 1984).

CHAPTER TWO

Science and Faith: A Continuing Battle?

God Himself is the best Poet,
And the Real is His Song.
Elizabeth Barrett Browning

O God, I am thinking Thy thoughts after Thee.
Johannes Kepler

Science, at bottom, is really anti-intellectual. It always distrusts pure reason and demands the production of objective fact.
H.L. Mencken

"Faith is a bunch of nonsense." He put down his coffee cup and settled back into his chair. He was a successful businessman whose hope in life was found in the computer industry. Science was his hobby; Carl Sagan was his hero.

He approached religion as though it were a bothersome remnant of ancient history. It irritated him that so many "good, thinking people" still believed that God had anything to do with the world.

Crossing his arms, he theorized, "This is the age of science. The day is coming when everyone will realize that true knowledge is only derived from science. We don't need to believe blindly in any pie-in-the-sky religious double-talk."

"Christianity is not based on futile speculation," I countered. "There are good reasons to believe—"

Interrupting, he leaned forward to emphasize his point. "I want *facts*, not *faith.*"

"But faith is just as valid as science," I protested.

But before I could explain, he grumbled, "Faith is nothing but an intellectual cop-out. You just don't want to face reality. Science is defiant to any kind of religion, and—" he paused and smiled, "one day will destroy it."

Drawing the Battle Lines

My agnostic friend's statement would receive a rousing "Amen" in some quarters and be shouted down in others. As many see it, our modern age is marked by a battle between science and religion, "fact" versus "faith." Both struggle to conquer the same intellectual territory, the origin of the universe and mankind's relationship to it. Yet the two approaches appear to be mutually exclusive with no middle ground, no room for compromise.

On one side, science is perceived as pushing our world forward, systematically uncovering once-unknown facts about ourselves and our world. Pioneer 10, launched in March 1972, continues on its journey out of our solar system to explore the regions beyond. Voyagers I and II, launched in 1977, have given us spectacular close-ups of Jupiter, Saturn, and Uranus, with more to come. Scientists claim that radio telescopes have discovered quasars over twelve *billion* light-years away.[1]

Scientists also peer into the atom to explore the vastness of inner space. At CERN, the atomic research center near Geneva, Switzerland, physicists smash together subatomic particles in a huge four-mile circular tunnel, attempting to discover the fundamental forces of life and matter. Plans are to spend over $4 billion to build a fifty-six-mile-long "atom smasher" in the United States. Indeed, technology advances at a dizzying pace, giving man the hope of ultimate dominion over his world.

Those who see science as the only way to true knowledge view religion as naive and oppressive, thwarting the inevitable advance of humanity. They believe the religious of today retreat into the superstitions of ancient writings and foist archaic standards of truth and morality on modern man. "Religionists" are caricatured as wide-eyed, book-burning, clinic-bombing fanatics who fear the advances of science like the primitive natives feared the jungle explorers' flashlights and watches.

On the other side of the battle line, many perceive religion as the last stronghold of truth and righteousness in a world careening out of control toward anarchy and chaos. According to these people, only belief in God and adherence to His Laws can keep mankind from destroying itself. They cast a jaundiced eye toward the advances of science. While acknowledging that scientific technology has made man's world easier and heightened his leisure, they quickly point out that the tragic result of this technology has been a dependence on, even an addiction to, gadgets and devices, taking man's eyes off spiritual needs and turning them to worldly pursuits.

Many of the religious feel that a preoccupation with scientific advancement is the cause of the moral decline of the Western world. They believe that science, at best, is a mixed bag of tricks—sometimes helpful, sometimes harmful. It has given us nuclear power but also nuclear weapons and waste; it has brought advances in medical treatment but also problematic procedures such as organ harvesting and genetic engineering. Only religion has the answers for humanity's ultimate concerns, and so religious pursuits must take precedence over every other pursuit.

The above descriptions are exaggerated, yet the tension between the two sides is real and continues to grow.

But does a battle truly exist between science and religion? Must we choose one or the other as the guiding principle for our lives? By believing in God, are Christians turning their backs on the "assured results" of science?

The answer to these questions is, of course, *no*. The battle between science and religion is more imagined than real, and to claim that the two are antagonistic is to misunderstand both. When each is placed in its proper role, the antagonism disappears. Christians can heartily join in the scientific search for knowledge without any fear of denying or damaging their faith. More important, Christians need not apologize for their faith. Belief for the Christian is neither a hurried retreat into superstition nor an unintellectual rejection of science; it is the acceptance of the biblical view of God and man that is authenticated by good evidence.

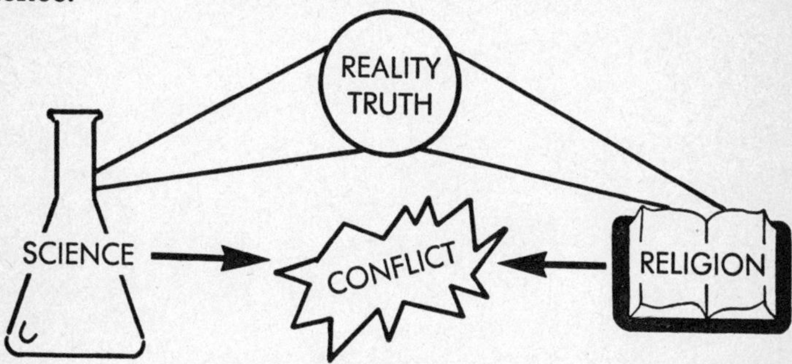

Fig. 1 The supposed battle between science and religion

Before we explore the actual content of the Christian faith, we must take a closer look at science. We must understand both the positive and negative effects of science on religion.

Science: Mankind's Pride and Joy

Our society is enamored with science. This is true for two reasons: science produces facts, and science helps us on a practical level.

We are a fact-oriented people. Like Joe Friday of "Dragnet," we want "just the facts, Ma'am." We enjoy the security and certainty that facts give us. Knowing that we like to make decisions based on the facts, politicians go on fact-finding trips to gather information about crucial issues. Facts are certain, objective, and shared by everyone.

Sometimes we may get carried away in our desire for "only the facts." Once as a young reporter, Mark Twain was instructed never to state as a fact anything that he could not personally verify. As a result, he wrote the following report describing a social event:

"A woman giving the name of Mrs. James Jones, who is reported to be one of the society leaders of the city, is said to have given what purported to be a party yesterday to a number of alleged ladies. The hostess claims to be the wife of a reputed attorney."[2]

One way facts are produced is the scientific method which involves: (1) observation (facts obtained by the five senses, i.e., "It is cold outside; I can see my breath"); and (2) experimentation (facts obtained by observing repeatable occurrences, i.e., "Water freezes at 0°C"). Most of us would agree that facts obtained by the careful usage of the scientific method can be accepted as certain truth. This method has been used to advance technology and medicine over the past century. From television and airplanes to cough syrup and Velcro fasteners, modern scientific discoveries permeate our work, our health, and our leisure.

We have come to view science as the pinnacle of man's achievements. Almost a superstitious belief exists that science has all the answers, or at least one day will find them. To observe this awe of science, just toss the term *scientific* into any argument or discussion and see what respect it commands. For example, not long ago I was listening to a discussion concerning the issue of sex education in high school. One of the panel experts stated that she felt sex education led to sexual experimentation by high school students and cited several examples. The panel expert who held an opposing view was asked to respond. He calmly replied, "I know of no scientific proof that sex education leads to sexual experimentation." Case closed!

Notice that he did not say there was no scientific proof, only that he did not know of any. In spite of his non-answer, other members of the panel explained that they considered his "scientific" response superior to the "opinion" of the other expert.

Sometimes the misuse of *scientific* borders on the absurd. Watching cartoons with my daughter one Saturday morning, I heard one of the characters state, "By the position of the stars and other signs, I have scientifically determined that tonight is the best night to catch a leprechaun!" The cartoon children oohed and ahhed with proper amazement at this revelation.

A second reason we are enamored with science is that, on the practical level, we are all scientists. Science is not limited to the sterile confines of the laboratory; we are engaged in scientific research every day. In order to exist in our world, we must live by the results of our own use of the scientific method. For example, by simple observation I can learn that it is raining outside, so I'll need my umbrella. I can also observe that I have a flat tire on my car which I must change before I can drive to work. By experimentation I have proven that when my wife drinks coffee, she gets sick, and that taking the expressway is usually the quickest way to the city.

Casual experimentation is usually the way we learn what is safe and what is not. One renowned scientist had a tendency to take it to absurd extremes. Early one morning he was walking along a forest trail with his young niece. Spotting a large, white mushroom growing just off the path, the little girl rushed to pick it. Holding it up to her uncle she asked hopefully, "Can I eat it?"

"Certainly," the scientist replied.

After she consumed the mushroom, the pair set off again down the trail. A few minutes later the uncle stopped and cast an inquiring gaze toward his niece. "How do you feel?" he asked.

"Fine," she answered.

"Good," the scientist replied with a grin. "Now we know another species of mushroom that is not poisonous!"

We all live by the results of our personal "scientific investigations." We must respond to these facts or at least make some provisions because of their existence. To ignore them would be foolhardy and even dangerous. The scientific method works for us every day at the practical level, giving us certain truths about ourselves and our world. Herein we find our kinship with professional scientists.

The Limitations of Science

As helpful as the scientific method is, we must always keep in mind that science is a limited venture in that it concerns itself with *observable* and *repeatable events* in the physical universe. It is nothing more than a *method* for obtaining knowledge. Yet this does not stop many people from making science into something it is not: a full-blown philosophy, explaining the universe and man's relationship to it. This philosophy, which is nothing more than secular religion, is best expressed by the term *naturalism*. Robert Jastrow, professor of astronomy and geology at Columbia University, agrees that believers in naturalism "have their own religion." He admits, "The principle element in that religion, or 'faith,' is a belief that everything that happens in the world has a scientific explanation."[3]

The tenets of naturalism are simple: (1) all reality is material; (2) every event within the universe can be explained by completely impersonal and natural causes.

Naturalism takes only one small facet of man's ability to understand the world (the scientific method) and reduces all reality and truth to whatever may be discovered by this single method.

Now it is true that the scientific method can produce a great deal of knowledge and certainty, but it is only one of many ways we obtain knowledge. Try to scientifically prove the following statements: "Murder is wrong," "I love you," "I feel great." Right away we see that observation and experimentation cannot help us understand many important and practical areas of our lives. It is one thing to say that science can give us knowledge, quite another to claim that science is the *only* way to obtain knowledge.

Imagine a man who was born without the ability to see, taste, hear, or smell. He has only the sense of touch by which to perceive the world. He can touch animals, furniture, trees, and people. He can sense warmth and cold, feel the vibrations of someone walking or speaking, and may even be able to communicate with his hands. But there are many experiences that he will never have. The smell of a flower, the sound of music, the taste of a hamburger, and the sight of a majestic mountain are all beyond his limited perception. This man's view of reality is reduced to that which he can touch.

Suppose this man were somehow to communicate that the sense of touch was the only legitimate means by which any of us could know reality. We would conclude that he was limiting others because of his own limitations.

In a similar way, naturalism reduces reality to only that which can be verified by the scientific method. But unlike the man with only the sense of touch, believers in naturalism *choose* to limit themselves—a choice that seems unwarranted not only to Christians, but to many scientists as well. Astronomer Jastrow acknowledges that science "is one avenue of truth. But it is clear to me it is not the only one."[4]

Science is limited in that it can prove *some* realities, not all. The Bible makes a clear distinction between realities which can be "seen" (scientifically provable) and those which cannot be seen (beyond scientific proof). The writer of Hebrews describes faith as "the conviction of things *not* seen" (Heb. 11:1), while the Apostle Paul states that faith allows us to "look not at the things which are seen, but at the things which are *not seen;* for the things which are seen are temporal, but the things which are *not seen* are eternal" (2 Cor. 4:18, emphasis added). The Bible does not teach that these "things which are not seen" oppose the "things which are seen"; rather, it seems to imply that the unseen realities go beyond that which is seen.

Seventeenth-century scientist and philosopher Blaise

Pascal summed it up well: "Faith indeed tells us what the senses do not tell, but not contrary of what they see. It is above them and not contrary to them."[5]

Science in Perspective

Faith and science are not enemies but allies. Albert Einstein once noted, "Religion without science is lame, but science without religion is blind."[6] Christians must work at understanding the partnership of faith and science.

Christians must recognize the true nature and role of science. First, science makes *basic assumptions* about the universe, and second, science is a *limited* enterprise.

Science assumes that the universe is a self-consistent, rational system that is dictated by a constant rule of cause-effect. These assumptions are what many called the "faith" of the scientific method. How many experiments could a scientist perform if he did not have faith in the accuracy of his instruments? What conclusions could he draw if he failed to assume that every observable effect has a discoverable cause?

Science is limited as a method of obtaining knowledge. It can only operate in the realm of the physical world and can say nothing about the existence of anything beyond. There is a big difference between the erroneous claim, "Science has proven that God does not exist," and the correct statement, "Science cannot prove or disprove the existence of God."

Furthermore, science is limited in that it cannot answer man's questions about his own purpose and the purpose of the universe. We may study a painting scientifically and determine its size and weight, the colors and quantity of the paint, and the angles of the brushstrokes. We may count and identify the various objects which are represented in the painting.

But only the artist himself can tell us why he painted the picture and what each of the objects represents. He can unlock the hidden meanings of the details and give us the intended overall effect of his work.

The scientific method can tell us the what and how about the painting or the universe, but it can't explain the *why.*

Christians must see scientific facts as part of a single fabric that encompasses all truth. We should welcome science as a partner in discovering truth about creation. Christianity is rooted in history and reality, not philosophical speculation; so science cannot be ignored.

Science describes the movement of the stars; the Bible describes the Star-maker. Science gives statistics about crime; the Bible reveals the reason for crime. Science tells us how we gain a little knowledge; the Bible tells us how we gain eternal life.

This perspective is reflected in the large number of prominent scientists who are strong believers in Christ. They see no contradiction between the teachings of Christ and the findings of scientific investigation. Just because a person is an advocate of the scientific method does not mean that he has rejected God. Stanford University professor Richard Bube quips, "There are probably as many atheistic truck drivers as atheistic scientists." Carnegie-Mellon physics professor Robert Griffiths adds, "If we need an atheist for a debate, I go to the philosophy department. The physics department isn't much use."[7]

Christians should use scientific truths more fully to understand the nature and character of God. Far from dismissing the presence of God, science has made the notion of God plausible. First, science points to the infinite power and order of the universe which reveal not only the existence of God but also His character. "For since the creation of the world His invisible attributes, His eternal power and divine nature, have been clearly seen, being understood through what has been made, so that they are without excuse" (Rom. 1:20).

Also, science points to the finitude of man, his smallness compared to the vastness of his universe. Yet deep within our being we know that we are more than insignificant specks. *We* look at the stars; they don't look at us. God has indeed put eternity in our hearts (see Ecc. 3:11).

Just as science endeavors to discover truth, our faith also must align itself with truth. Does it really matter *what* I believe? The answer, of course, is *yes*. There is no virtue in believing something that is wrong, no matter how sincere and strong our faith might be.

For this reason, let us turn our attention to the content of our faith. In the next chapter we will see that the dynamic quality of true faith is present only if we believe the truth.

Discussion Questions

1. Why does there seem to be a battle between science and religion?

2. What is meant by the statement: "Science is a limited enterprise"? In what ways is it limited?

3. Why are we so enamored with science and technology?

4. Discuss the differences between science and naturalism. How are the two often confused in popular thinking?

5. How does "faith" relate to science?

6. Discuss the statement: "Science cannot prove that God exists; therefore, God does not exist."

Further Reading

Michael D. Aeschliman, *The Restitution of Man: C.S. Lewis and the Case against Naturalism* (Grand Rapids: William B. Eerdmans, 1983).

Carl F. Henry, editor, *Horizons of Science: Christian Scholars Speak Out* (San Francisco: Harper and Row, 1978).

Arthur Holmes, editor, *The Making of a Christian Mind* (Downers Grove, Ill.: InterVarsity Press, 1985).

Bernard Ramm, *The Christian View of Science and Scripture* (Grand Rapids: William B. Eerdmans, 1954).

CHAPTER THREE

Isn't Sincerity Enough?

Unless he believes rightly, there is not the faintest reason why he should believe at all. And in that case it is wholly irrelevant to chatter about "Christian principles."

Dorothy Sayers

There are two ways to slide easily through life: to believe everything or to doubt everything; both ways save us from thinking.

Alfred Korzybski

The attainment of truth indeed is the function of every part of the intellect.

Artistotle

Four people sit under sweltering lights before a studio audience of several hundred and a television audience of several million. Each person represents a different view of today's controversial subject: controlling AIDS. After ten minutes of introducing the issues involved in the subject, one of the guests concludes his plans for controlling the spread of the disease with the following statement: "The best way to fight AIDS in our country is to encourage abstinence."

"Whoa, wait a minute!" The show's host, standing in the aisle among the studio participants, waves one hand while holding a microphone in the other. "Are you going to push your view of morality on other people?"

Another guest speaks up. "It's more than a matter of views—it's a matter of right and wrong. There are—"

"Oh, I see," the host interrupts. "You're telling me what's right and what's wrong. Who made you God, buddy?"

"I'm not claiming to be God, but some lifestyles are clearly wrong."

"Clear to whom? It's not clear to me. Is it clear to you?" He sweeps his arm toward the studio audience. Heads gesture in all directions. He turns to face the stage. "I have just as much right as you to determine the way I want to live. But I don't go around forcing my lifestyle on others. You're problem is that you are so narrow-minded that you think your opinions should be everybody's opinions. Well, I'm not buying it."

The audience applauds. The "open" discussion continues.

Such television shows are popular forums for some of today's major issues and problems. While many of the subjects covered border on the absurd, an underlying current of relativism permeates the discussions and the treatment of the guests. The only allowable "truth" is that all people have the right to believe whatever they want. The only sin is to claim that "my views are right" and "your views are wrong." This is made patently clear not only when moral issues are discussed but also when religious questions are raised.

"So you are telling me that there is only one way to get to heaven?" The host rolled his eyes toward the audience. "And that way is by believing in Jesus and 'getting saved,' right?"

The guest tugged at his collar. He knew what was coming, but he answered honestly. "Yes, that is what the Bible says."

"Where do you people get off thinking that you are the only ones who can interpret the Bible? I've read the Bible; I didn't get that out of it."

"Jesus Himself said, 'I am the way, the truth, and the life; no one comes to the Father but through Me.'"

"But what about a guy who believes in God and lives a good moral life—I mean a life like the Bible describes, not the kind of hypocrisy that we've seen from these television preachers—what happens to him? Is God going to send him to hell just because he never 'got saved'?"

"I can't answer a hypothetical question like that," the guest stated. "All I know is what God has said in His Word."

"There are a lot of Bibles around." The host laughed. "Which one? I think it doesn't matter what you believe as long as you are sincere and love your fellowman."

The audience applauded.

For many people, as long as someone acknowledges the existence of God or lives a moral life, then that person has done all that could be expected. It does not matter *what* a person believes.

The Apostle Paul took a different view. He grieved over the Israelites' failure to believe God's revealed truth. In spite of their sincerity and moral lifestyle, Paul saw them as outside God's redemptive plan:

> Brethren, my heart's desire and my prayer to God for them is for their salvation. For I bear them witness that they have a zeal for God, but not in accordance with knowledge. For not knowing about God's righteousness, and seeking to establish their own, they did not subject themselves to the righteousness of God. For Christ is the end of the law for righteousness to everyone who believes" (Rom. 10:1-4).

Paul acknowledged the Israelites had a "zeal for God." Yet, in spite of their sincerity and zeal, they were believing the wrong things.

But how do we know what the truth is? Many different views of the world and life clamor for the right to be called the "correct view."

What Are the Options?

So many people claim to have answers to the mystery of the universe and our existence. We are faced with many options. The major views generally fall into one of three groups: naturalism, pantheism, or theism.

	View of God	**View of the Universe**	**View of Humanity**	**View of the Future**
Naturalism	No God	Always existed	Product of physical processes	Nothing beyond the grave
Pantheism (Eastern thought)	All reality is "God"	Equated with God	Spirits imprisoned in bodies	Reincarnation or impersonal existence
Theism	Personal God	Created by God	Created in God's image	Eternal, personal existence

Fig. 2 Worldview options

The chart above is not intended to ignore the complexities of these views. There are, of course, many variations which would not fit into the general explanations above. The chart simply presents the major tenets of each view. We need to take a closer look at these views.

Naturalism: "What You See Is All There Is"

"The cosmos is all that is or ever was or ever will be." This statement, made by Carl Sagan on his popular "Cosmos" television program, sums up the essential features of naturalism (which I mentioned in chapter 2): the belief that all of reality is contained in the physical world and that no forces or beings exist beyond the observable universe. What you see is all there is.

The Marquis de Laplace (1749–1827) was a brilliant

mathematician and astronomer in France. For almost thirty years he researched and calculated the universal effects of gravity. The result of his study was a massive five-volume work, *Celestial Mechanics*, published in 1827.

Laplace presented a copy of his work to Napoleon who studied it carefully. Sending for Laplace, Napoleon stated, "You have written a large book about the universe without once mentioning the author of the universe."

"Sire," the scientist replied, "I have no need of that hypothesis."[1]

For Laplace, and other philosophical naturalists, the universe is a huge clock, ticking along with no need of any outside help. The "God-hypothesis" is an unnecessary intrusion into the assured results of scientific investigation. Even man himself, as part of the cosmic clock, is nothing more than an evolved contraption. The human machine begins to function at birth and ceases at death—the grave is the end.

Things are as they are completely by chance. Every event in the universe, from the cosmic explosion of a supernova to the tear of a small child, is explained as a result of random and physical processes. Even our thoughts and personalities are described as electrical impulses or secretions of our brains.

For the believer in naturalism, *all reality* is found in matter and, therefore, *all truth* may be discovered by the scientific method. If something cannot be measured, weighed, or otherwise "scientifically proven," then naturalism throws it out as meaningless.

From the point of view of modern naturalism, those who have faith are seen as either ignorant or lazy and unaware of the "hard facts" produced by the scientific method. Whereas science offers proof, faith can never prove anything beyond doubt, so the believer is often accused of being unintellectual, naive, or even dishonest.

Naturalism regards faith not as an expression of the way things are but as an opinion or wish. For example, when I say, "I believe in God" naturalism claims that I'm really saying, "In my opinion there is a God, even though it cannot be proven," or "I hope there is a God." Because no experiment scientifically supports the statement "I believe in God," naturalism suggests that all discussions about the existence of God are absurd and meaningless.

At the practical level, naturalism is the most popular of the worldviews. If there is no God or life after death, then I am the master of my own fate. I give account to no one. I alone decide what is right or wrong and what I will do with my life.

Pantheism: "God Is All and All Is God"

"The reason I have such anxiety," she explained, "is that in my former life I was an Egyptian princess during the reign of a cruel Pharaoh." I chuckled at what I thought was a joke. It wasn't. My friend further detailed her belief in mankind's immortality and the hope of reincarnation. "The new age shall come when mankind will be one," she promised.

This woman's thinking has been shaped by the popular New Age movement, a new breeze blowing through the Western world which promises peace and unity for all people. This new breeze is really the old wind of pantheism, the belief that all is God and God is all. God is viewed as a personal force, not a personal being. There is no God outside the universe because the universe *is* God. Historically, pantheism has wound its way through Western philosophers such as Plotinus (circa A.D. 205–270) and Spinoza (1632–1677) and has been the worldview underpinning most Eastern religions.

Modern expressions of pantheism are popularized in movies (*Star Wars* and *E.T.*), children's cartoons ("He Man" and the "Masters of the Universe"), and business seminars (est and FORUM).

Evidence of the tremendous influence of New Age thought is present everywhere. Thousands of New Agers met on August 16, 1987 at selected places around the world for a "Harmonic Convergence." People held hands and chanted in an attempt to synchronize the earth with the rest of the galaxy and bring about a new era of peace.

The television special by Shirley MacLaine has given prime time exposure to many New Age beliefs. Her writings endorse such activities as channeling, yoga, reincarnation, UFO contacts, and the occult. In her book *Dancing in the Light,* she proclaims, "Everyone is God. Everyone." In her later book, *It's All in the Playing,* she describes her self-imposed divinity which occupied her thoughts as she walked down a Hollywood street: "I created everything I saw, heard, touched, smelled, tasted, everything I loved, hated, revered . . . I created everything I knew."[2]

Borrowing heavily from Eastern thought, the New Age gospel preaches that all life is unified. From the lowest living cell to the highest form of existence, we are all part of the universal force called "life." It is merely seen in different forms. Nothing is greater than this force within us; therefore, we are all "God." Our problems, we are taught, are the result of our ignorance of this fact. New Agers also believe that each individual must work to overcome the consequences of mistakes made in past lives because this bad karma keeps a person enslaved to the continuing cycle of rebirth until personal enlightenment comes to free him from bondage.

New Age philosophy teaches that enlightened "Masters" such as Hercules, Buddha, and Jesus have appeared throughout history to point the way to personal enlightenment and universal harmony. A new "Christ" is expected soon and will lead us to a new era of worldwide peace, the "Aquarian Age."

New Agers hope to hasten the arrival of the new era by becoming involved in social concerns, such as nuclear disarmament, human equality, wildlife preservation, and ecological concerns, which promote peace and unity.

The promises of modern pantheism are enticing. Pantheists suggest that when we become aware of the fact that we are "God," then we become the master of our own fate. We must simply tap into the divinity within us and harness it to our advantage. Because of the unity of all things, "tuning in" to our own divinity can bring about success and prosperity in this life. A recent *Wall Street Journal* article described individuals who "chanted" certain phrases which activated the "positive energy" within them to obtain everything from cars and jobs to better seats at a concert.[3]

Pantheism, like naturalism, is an inviting explanation of the universe because it encourages each person to be his own creator and redeemer.

Theism: "God Is, and the Universe Is His"

French novelist André Gide once admitted, "It is much more difficult than one thinks not to believe in God."[4] Man's religious spirit is pervasive throughout history. Even secular sociologists agree that "religion exists in every known society."[5] Why? Theism teaches that man's persistent religious nature is a reflection of the image of God in which man was created.

Whereas naturalism and pantheism reject the existence of a God who is separate from the physical universe, traditional theism holds to the reality of a personal God who is both outside the universe and also within it. All things were created by Him and are dependent on Him for their continued existence. Theism holds that belief in a rational God explains the rational order of the universe; belief in a personal God explains the personality and character of man.

Because theists believe that mankind is a special object of God's creative love and constant care, they also believe that man is not the master of his own fate or the shaper of his own standard of morality and truth. Questions concerning premarital sex or pornography or abortion are not answered by man's decisions but by God's decrees.

The three major monotheistic religions—Christianity, Judaism, and Islam—all follow the basic tenets of theism. All three promote belief in a personal God who created the world and who is actively involved in the activities of man. Judaism holds to the view of God revealed in the Old Testament and interpreted by later Jewish teachers in the Talmud. Followers of Islam express their allegiance to God by accepting the Bible as a revelation from Him but corrected and amended by the prophet Muhammad (A.D. 570–632). Christianity, however, departs drastically from the others for one reason: belief in the Person of Jesus Christ. We will take up the significance of this belief and the uniqueness of Christ in chapter 7.

Choosing Belief or Unbelief

Now, we can draw several conclusions from our study of the above explanations:

1. All of the worldviews require acceptance by faith. That is, no experiment can be performed to demonstrate the truth or falsity of any explanation.
2. All of the worldviews attempt to answer the same basic questions about man's existence.
3. Each worldview excludes the others and sets itself up as being *the* truth while declaring the others false. The views are mutually exclusive.

Our conclusions about naturalism, pantheism, and theism raise unsettling questions. If each of these explanations is "scientifically unprovable," does it really matter what we believe? Doesn't a person have the right to believe whatever he wants? Shouldn't sincerity count for something?

Who is right? Is there any way to know that *I'm* right about what I believe? Others will always have good reasons to believe the exact opposite.

Because of the disturbing questions raised by the variety of options, many have thrown up their hands and declared that what a person believes is not important. Like someone who cuts off his head to get rid of dandruff, many people have completely dismissed the value of belief because of a few itchy problems. This surrender to despair takes two opposite approaches.

The Agnostic Approach

Agnostics claim *nobody* has the right answers to the ultimate questions. While they will admit, "Sure, we want to know why we are here and where we are going," they concede that the answers to such questions are beyond us. So agnostics encourage us not to worry about what we cannot know but to be concerned with what we DO know: ourselves. Many agnostics also appeal to science as the only rightful criteria of what is true and false.

Fred claimed to be an agnostic. He was not opposed to Christians or atheists—he felt they were free to believe whatever they wanted. "My life is fine just as it is," he professed. "Maybe there's a God and maybe there isn't. He hasn't done anything for me one way or another. I just want to make the most out of my life and so far I've done just fine without having to worry about God."

It is fashionable now to be a skeptic and an agnostic. In fact, a California organization, the Society of Evangelical Agnostics (SEA), has been formed with the expressed purpose of spreading the "good news of agnosticism."[6] The good news they spread is that people do not have to make decisions about the riddle of the universe and man's existence. No person is expected to have a final answer.

The agnostics' response to every meaningful question is "Who knows?" Even if we were to ask, "Do you know that agnosticism is the right approach?" again, the agnostic must shrug and answer, "Who knows?" He would rather search for truth than find it. Why? Finding truth demands a decision—a decision an agnostic does not want to make.

The Therapeutic Approach

The therapeutic approach claims that *everyone* has the right answers to the ultimate questions. The answers are discovered by personal reflection and then believed because of the benefit to the believer.

"It's not what you believe that's important, but what your faith does for you," a pastor told me. He considers himself a "therapist," one who helps people get in touch with their feelings and feel good about themselves. For him, faith is only a personal, emotional activity which gives us a deeper understanding of ourselves and our lives. We are justified in believing whatever we want as long as it results in making us better people.

In this view, faith is not directed toward a higher being but focused inward, becoming psychological exercise solely to benefit the one doing the believing.

This understanding of faith and truth leaves us spiritually and intellectually stranded. While it is true that psychological benefits do accompany faith, to reduce faith to an inward, reflective, and reflexive activity is the height of absurdity.

Imagine for a moment that I truly believe that the earth is flat (with the hearty approval from the members of the Flat Earth Society!), After gathering a certain amount of information, I am fully convinced that the earth is not a sphere but a huge flat chunk of rock. This belief makes me feel good and takes away the fear I had of flying off a spinning globe.

Am I justified in my faith? Those who follow the therapeutic approach and see faith as merely a psychological exercise would say yes. They would ignore what my faith says about the shape of the world and point out that my faith gives me a sense of security and happiness.

Those who follow either the agnostic approach or the therapeutic approach neatly avoid definitive answers to the ultimate questions. Does it really matter what we believe about life and death and God? The answer, of course, is yes.

We must come to some conclusion about the existence of God and our own personal future; this is not optional. Either God exists, or He doesn't; either heaven exists, or it doesn't; either Jesus Christ is the only way to God, or He isn't. *Refusing* to decide is a major decision in itself. We cast our lot by decision or default.

Christianity Compared to Other Worldviews

Frank was a math major at a large university. The final exam for his calculus class consisted of one problem which involved using a number of theorems he had memorized. After carefully recording the theorems at the beginning of the problem, he plowed through eight pages of calculations before he finally put down his pen. Confident he had done well, he turned in his exam and went home to rest his brain.

The next week when he received his graded exam, he was horrified to discover how poorly he had done. Page after page of red ink dispelled any hope of getting a good grade. Where had he gone wrong? On the first page, at the beginning of the problem he found his error. He had misstated a crucial theorem. That small error changed the truth of the theorem. Though he had performed the calculations correctly, the error at the beginning of the problem resulted in an incorrect answer.

Errors at the beginning of some things are not always as fatal. The stumbling start of a hurdler does not ruin the entire event. The mistake can be compensated for by a staggered step.

Truth is not so. Errors of belief, like a mislaid cornerstone, have a constant and dangerous effect on the superstructure. *What* we believe is crucial because it sets the course for *how* we live.

Comparing the Christian worldview to the alternate views presented earlier reveals the contrast between the views and the dangerous results of holding to either naturalism or pantheism.

NATURALISM: A LIMITED VIEW OF REALITY

Naturalism provides a very limited view of reality. Well-known physicist Stephen Hawking once remarked, "When I was a boy I wanted to know how and why the universe worked. Now I know how, but I don't know why."[7] Hawking's statement reveals a basic inadequacy of naturalism as a full-blown worldview dependent on science. It can usually tell us *how* something, such as the law of gravity or the electromagnetic force works, but not *why* it works.

As we discussed in chapter 2, naturalism fails to account for realities which go beyond the material world. The Bible clearly reveals that there are "eternal things" which are not seen (2 Cor. 4:18).

The greatest deficiency of naturalism is in its moral implications. If this life is all there is, then why should I lay aside my desires in the interest of anyone else? After all, my short life has no ultimate purpose, nor do I have any responsibility for my actions. It would appear that anything that heightens the enjoyment of my own life should be allowed.

For this reason, "quality of life" replaces "sanctity of life." Abortion, infanticide, and euthanasia become not only accepted but encouraged if they enhance the quality of one's life. Sex without guilt, success without ethics—there are no barriers in the pursuit of "having it all."

For all its appeal to scientific certainty and moral freedom, naturalism leads ultimately to a despair of the human situation. Life becomes at best a meaningless existence and at worst a bad cosmic joke.

Pantheism: Man Worshiping Himself

Pantheism, as expressed by New Age thought, is an enchanting worldview. Positive thinking, unity among all people, and a future of eternal peace give hope in a world of despair. Many of the social concerns which are by-products of New Age thought closely follow the biblical commands to aid the oppressed and needy.

But as a worldview, modern pantheism leaves too many unanswered questions. New Age thought fails to explain how individual personalities can arise from an impersonal force. Describing evil as merely "man's ignorance of his own divinity" does not deal with the reality of the human situation. The problem is not perception but admission of personal evil.

Further, a biblical worldview in no way allows for reincarnation. While the Bible acknowledges that man is immortal, his incarnation is a one-time event: "And inasmuch as it is appointed for men to die once and after this comes judgment" (Heb. 9:27).

New Age theology also fails to take into account the historical record of Jesus Christ. His life and teachings do not allow Him to be considered as one among many "enlightened masters." He presented Himself uniquely and exclusively as the incarnate God who alone created and sustained the universe (John 1:3; Col. 1:16) and provided the way of personal salvation (John 14:6; Acts 4:12).

Pantheism is a most difficult worldview to confront because it promises progressive and universal salvation. It is the most natural of human religions because it is too good to be true. The spiritual bankruptcy of pantheism leaves a void in the heart of man. But man's infatuation with himself will not allow him to judge himself to be sinful and in need of a savior. So rather than looking outward and worshiping the Creator, he has turned inward and worshiped the creature (Rom. 1:25). Pantheism is the ultimate self-worship: it takes away man's depravity and replaces it with divinity.

Christianity: An Extraordinary Worldview

Naturalism and pantheism are the kind of worldview we would expect to arise in the mind of man. But biblical Christianity does not give us a "natural" worldview created by human beings. As C.S. Lewis concluded, Christianity "is not the sort of thing anyone would have made up. It has just that queer twist about it that real things have."[8]

Christianity says that all things belong to God. The universe around us and the conscience within us reveal the thumbprint of the omnipotent, good, and personal God. Christians believe that mankind is alienated from God because of sin. By God's initiative, the relationship between God and mankind is restored through the reconciling atonement of His own Son. Human beings are only at peace when they are rightly related to their Creator.

For the world, Christianity offers purpose and meaning. Those who embrace Christ personally have hope for this life and the life to come.

Christians believe that their worldview best explains the world around them and satisfies the needs within all of us.

Evangelical Immunity?

Before we turn our attention to some of the specifics of the Christian faith, we must take a brief moment for personal evaluation. If believing correctly is so important, then we would assume that evangelical Christians, fully convinced of the correctness of their faith, would value and promote the teaching of that truth. But this is not always the case.

Evangelical Christians are not immune from any disregard for truth. Within the context of the church, many have jettisoned the emphasis upon the biblical truth and now rely on other avenues of truth. Many disturbing trends hinder the teachings of correct doctrine.

The first of these trends is *pragmatism:* truth is measured by what works. A pastor noted, "I've got people in my church that don't believe in the Trinity or that Jesus is God; but hey, God is blessing." His church building is full on Sunday morning and the fellowship is dynamic. Why worry about doctrine when the numbers are good?

A second trend hindering the teaching of correct doctrine is *existentialism:* doctrine is determined by subjective interpretation. Truth depends on an individual's interpretation of it. "We haven't had a sermon in our church for two months," one woman proudly proclaimed to me. "We've just been worshiping the Lord in our own way every Sunday morning."

A third trend is *anti-intellectualism:* any systematic study of doctrine stifles the true work of the Spirit.

A college student once warned me of the "dangerous doctrine of demons"—his description of systematic theology. "The Lord has given us the Holy Spirit to interpret Scripture," he explained. "Teaching doctrine is Satan's attempt to use our minds to understand the Bible rather than relying on the Holy Spirit."

The present undercurrent of anti-intellectualism is riding the momentum of nineteenth-century revivalism, which cast a jaundiced eye toward intellectual enterprises. Christians must learn to love God with their *minds* as well as their hearts and souls. The truth of God, as revealed in the Scriptures, is a treasure which must be both guarded and invested in the lives of people (2 Tim. 1:14; 2:1-2).

The study of doctrine has often been misrepresented as dull and uninteresting. This is the fault of Christians who are lazy thinkers and teachers who are poor communicators. How can the whole drama of the Creator God communicating with man and then becoming a man Himself be dull?

A continuing, vibrant study of the Bible is the soil from which Christian thinking grows. Good theology guards against the extreme errors so often found among Christians today. For example, the Bible informs us of God's standards for success: faithfulness and godliness (Matt. 25:14-30; 1 Thes. 4:3). A full church building is not necessarily a sign of God's blessings, nor is a small group an indication that something is wrong. Furthermore, the Bible cautions us against teachings which appeal only to our emotional desires (2 Tim. 4:3-4) and urges us to be nourished "on the words of the faith and of the sound doctrine" (1 Tim. 4:6).

Learning doctrine, however, is not an end in itself, but a means to understand and live the truth. "The goal of our instruction is love from a pure heart and a good conscience and a sincere faith" (1 Tim. 1:5).

All Christians are theologians. The question is whether we will be good theologians or bad ones.

Discussion Questions

1. Respond to the following statements: "It doesn't matter what you believe as long as you are sincere. Besides, all religions are the same."

2. "Agnosticism is the most humanitarian of all worldviews." Why would many people agree with this statement? How does it reflect the common approach to truth in our society?

3. Discuss the following statements:
   a. "Naturalism is too limited to give us the whole truth."
   b. "Pantheism is too good to be true."
   c. "Christianity is too narrow-minded."

4. Why do you feel most Christians are not interested in studying doctrine?

5. Are there elements of pragmatism, existentialism, or anti-intellectualism in your life? In your church or fellowship group? Are these elements *always* wrong?

Further Reading

R.C. Sproul, *Reason to Believe* (Grand Rapids: Zondervan Publishing House, 1978).

Herman Bavinck, *The Certainty of Faith* (St. Catharines, Ontario: Paideia Press, 1980).

Keith E. Yandell, *Christianity and Philosophy* (Grand Rapids: William B. Eerdmans, 1984).

Erwin Lutzer, *The Necessity of Ethical Absolutes* (Grand Rapids: Zondervan Publishing House, 1981).

William Dyrness, *Christian Apologetics in a World Community* (Downers Grove, Ill.: InterVarsity Press, 1980).

PART TWO:
THE BASIC BELIEFS OF CHRISTIANITY

CHAPTER FOUR

Why Believe in God?

In spite of all the yearnings of men, no one can produce a single fact or reason to support the belief in God and in personal immortality.
Clarence Darrow

To believe in God is impossible—not to believe in Him is absurd.
Voltaire

Two things fill the mind with ever new and increasing wonder and awe—the starry heavens above me, and the moral law within me.
Immanuel Kant

How can I believe in God when just last week I got my tongue caught in the roller of an electric typewriter?
Woody Allen

Over 90 percent of Americans believe in a Supreme Being. Even in what many consider the spiritually dark countries of Europe, a majority acknowledge a belief in God.

On the broader scale, almost three fifths of the world's population adheres to some form of belief in a single, personal God. Only one in every twenty-five people is a professing atheist.

These statistics, says *World Christian Encyclopedia* editor David Barrett, further reveal that Christian Theism is the single largest religion, claiming 1.64 billion adherents.[1] Such overwhelming numbers lend support to George Gallup's tongue-in-cheek claim, "I could prove God statistically."

Arguments against the Existence of God

While a large percentage of the world's population appears to believe in God, we must take note of the many people who choose not to admit that God exists. Many people refuse to believe in God for personal reasons, such as wanting to live life without any outside interference. Their desire to be self-sufficient and independent drives them away from God. Like teenagers rebelling against parental authority, they want to be their own boss and determine their own fate.

Bodybuilder and actor Arnold Schwarzenegger is a good example of a person who laid aside his search for God because of a desire to follow his own goals. As a fifteen-year-old budding athlete, Schwarzenegger was urged by a friend, Helmut Knaur, to give up going to church.

"Helmut insisted that if I achieved something in life, I shouldn't thank God for it; I should thank myself. It was the same thing if something bad happened. I shouldn't ask God for help. I should help myself. He asked me if I'd ever prayed for my body. I confessed I had. He said if I wanted a great body, I had to build it. Nobody else could. Least of all God.

"These were wild ideas for someone as young as I was. But they made perfect sense, and I announced to my family that I would no longer go to church, that I didn't believe in it and didn't have time to waste on it."[2]

In addition to these personal denials, many also question the existence of God because of two difficult issues: the presence of evil in the world, and the nature of man's mental limitations.

The Problem of Evil

Atheists may be a small minority, but they are a vocal minority who ask disturbing questions: Why is there evil in the world? If God is such a good and powerful God, why do so many innocent people suffer? Why do "evil" people prosper while "good" people experience distress?

The strongest argument against the existence of God does not come from science or psychology, but from the presence of evil in our world. The argument goes like this:

- An all-powerful God COULD destroy evil.
- A good and loving God WOULD destroy evil.
- But, evil is not destroyed;
- therefore, either God is not all-powerful and loving—or there is no God at all.

How can we refute this argument? How can we explain the presence of evil, defined as perverted good, in God's creation?

God created humanity with the express purpose of loving Him, but He also created humanity with the ability to choose. God does not want mindless automatons serving Him. Evil came into the world as a result of man's choice to love something other than God. The hearts of men turned to exalt themselves and their own desires, ignoring God. The result is every form of evil imaginable. By giving man the choice to reject Him, God has indirectly allowed evil to come into being.

One of the remarkable characteristics of the Bible is its honest portrayal of the human situation. The problem of evil is not ignored or glossed over with religious double-talk; it is met head-on. For example, the writer of Psalm 73 admits to second thoughts about his own commitment to the Lord when he sees how the wicked seem to prosper. "Surely in vain I have kept my heart pure, and washed my hands in innocence; For I have been stricken all day long, and chastened every morning" (Ps. 73:13-14).

The psalmist has trouble understanding why God does not destroy evil men but instead lets them prosper. Eventually, the writer of this psalm comes to understand the presence of evil in the world as he gains a perspective of the ultimate fate of the wicked. "I came into the sanctuary of God; then I perceived their [the wicked] end. Surely Thou dost set them in slippery places; Thou dost cast them down to destruction" (Ps. 73:17-18).

From our perspective, it may appear that evil has the upper hand. From God's perspective, evil is only temporary. It will be destroyed. A time is coming when justice will prevail and good will triumph.

Every Christian should take the time to think through the issues related to the reality of evil in our world. Several good books which discuss the problem of evil are listed in the suggested reading at the end of this chapter.

The story is told of a farmer in a Midwestern state who had a strong disdain for "religious" things. As he plowed his fields on Sunday morning, he would shake his fist at the church people who passed by on their way to worship.

October came and the farmer had his finest crop ever—the best in the entire county. When the harvest was complete, he placed an advertisement in the local paper which belittled the Christians for their faith in God. Near the end of his diatribe he wrote, "Faith in God must not mean much if someone like me can prosper."

The response from the Christians in the community was quiet and polite. In the next edition of the town paper, a small ad appeared at the bottom of page two. It read simply, "God doesn't always settle His accounts in October."

The Problem of Mankind's Limitations

Agnostics will claim that if God does exist, He would be so far beyond our ability to understand that we should have no hope of ever knowing anything about Him.

"How can an infinite God be understood by a finite human?" The answer to this question is twofold.

First, *Christians have never claimed to know everything about God.* Since when must we know everything about a person to say that we know him? We can know a person meaningfully without knowing him comprehensively. In other words, there are degrees of knowing another person. Certainly we know some people better than others; I know my wife much better than I know my colleagues at the college or the people at my church. But I still *know* these other people meaningfully without knowing them comprehensively. In a similar way, but on a grander scale, Christians can claim to know God because they have accepted what He has revealed about Himself. In no way can God be completely comprehended, but He can be known.

Second, the knowledge we have of God is not the result of painstaking search and speculation. Whatever we know about God has been revealed to us by God Himself. Christians do not claim to have found God; rather *we claim that God has found us*. "Because that which is known about God is evident within them; for God made it evident to them" (Rom. 1:19). If God had not revealed Himself, we would have no hope of ever truly knowing Him.

The arguments against the existence of God—the problem of evil and the problem of mankind's limitations—are not substantial enough to keep us from honestly evaluating the evidence for God's existence.

So now we come to the question, How do we know that God exists?

The Arguments for the Existence of God

"Prove to me that God exists."

Steve, the student to whom I had directed the challenge, squirmed in his seat and then finally answered, "I know that God exists because I talked to Him this morning."

"Did God answer you?" I asked.

"Sure," Steve replied. "God always hears the prayers of His children."

"What did He say to you?"

"Well, God doesn't actually use words. He communicates by feelings."

I smiled. "Oh, so God can't speak in words?"

Steve was getting serious. "No, God can speak in words, but it's different now . . . I mean . . . well, it's a feeling deep inside."

'Like the feeling you get after you eat a green enchilada?"

Steve grimaced. When the class laughter died down, he stated, "I just always assumed God existed. I never questioned it. Why do I have to prove it?"

Steve is not wrong in assuming that God exists. The Bible itself assumes the existence of God from the first words: "In the beginning God" (Gen. 1:1) to the final words: "The grace of our Lord Jesus be with all. Amen" (Rev. 22:21).

Despite the validity of his assumption, Steve is not absolved from the responsibility of knowing the arguments for the existence of God. Why? Many people need to cross an intellectual bridge before they can look to God. We must be prepared to give intelligent arguments for the existence of God. We must know how to help intellectuals take the first step in coming to God: believing that He exists (Heb. 11:6).

For our discussion of the existence of God, we will focus on the answers to questions concerning the existence and nature of the universe and humanity.

The Universe: *How was it created?*

The universe exists.

"Big deal," someone may say. "That's obvious."

But when we ask why the universe exists, things are not so clear.

Many skeptics have tried to answer this question by stating, "The universe just exists." But somehow we are not satisfied with such an answer. We want to know what caused the universe to exist. Can something come from nothing? We know that all we see in everyday experience has been caused to exist. Children do not just pop into existence. Snow does not suddenly spring up in the desert. A reasonable cause is present for every effect. When we begin to view the universe as an effect, we are forced to seek for a cause. All of creation practically screams with the news that it was formed and fashioned by God (Ps. 19:1). In everyday life when we see evidence of design, we automatically assume that someone was responsible. Not to make this assumption seems absurd, even humorous.

As I drove south through Georgia one summer, my family and I anticipated our arrival into Florida. Crossing the state border, we saw a group of flowers on a hillside arranged to spell "Welcome to Florida."

Let's suppose I had turned to my wife and said, "Isn't it amazing that those flowers grew in such a pattern at this precise place? I imagine that the odds of this occurring are astronomical—but there they are!"

My wife probably would have looked at me strangely and then checked to see if I had a fever.

When an agnostic or atheist claims that the universe is "just there," it sounds just as improbable as my words would have sounded to my wife.

Many consider the design argument to be the strongest clue to the existence of God. One of the most famous expressions of this approach was given by William Paley (1743–1805). He pointed out that if we found a watch lying on the ground, we would naturally assume that it had been constructed by a watchmaker. Instruments with such precision in design and function do not just occur at random. Paley applies this analogy to the universe and concludes that the universe must have been constructed by a Maker.[3]

Those who support the design argument argue that everything in the universe points to the existence of a Creator. They believe that everything, from the intricate biological functions of the human body to the behavior of stars and planets as they conform to the various laws of nature, implies the existence of God.

Bertrand Russell tried to dispense with the argument from design. When scientists look into the heavens, he claimed, they no longer must appeal to God to understand why planets revolve around the sun. The law of gravity explains it.[4]

But Russell misses the whole point of the design argument. The law of gravity may describe the way planets behave, but who created the law of gravity?

The best answer to the order and design present in our world is that an intelligent Orderer is responsible for all that we see. The intelligent design of the universe suggests that the universe did not just "happen."

An atheist cannot say, "I didn't know God because the evidence just was not clear enough." The Scriptures declare that to deny God is to reject the evidence God has made known: "For since the creation of the world His invisible attributes, His eternal power and divine nature, have been clearly seen, being understood through what has been made, so that they are without excuse" (Rom. 1:20).

We must acknowledge that these arguments for the existence of God do not prove the God of the Bible. At best they suggest a "First Cause" or what Aristotle called an "Unmoved Mover." But the evidence for God does not stop here.

When we ponder humanity, God's highest creation, we become further convinced that God exists.

HUMANITY: *Why are we like we are?*

Ronald Knox, British theologian and writer, was engaged in a theological discussion with scientist John Scott Haldane. "In a universe containing millions of planets," reasoned Haldane, "is it not inevitable that life should appear on at least one of them?"

"Sir," replied Knox, "if the police found a body in your cabin trunk, would you tell them: 'There are millions of trunks in the world—surely one of them must contain a body?' I think they would still want to know who put it there."[5]

The existence of life in the universe is one of God's most obvious calling cards. A cold, lifeless universe seems to be the natural result of a strictly physical view of the world—but here we are! Furthermore, when we examine the unique qualities of humanity, we discover even more evidence which clearly points to the existence of God.

Every human being has a unique *personality*. I see myself as an individual, distinct and unique. I have a mind, will, and emotions. I have the ability to think and experience emotion. I am me. I am the only me that has ever, or will ever, exist.

Mankind alone has the ability to be *creative*. We can make up stories about events that have never occurred, paint pictures of objects that do not exist, and even put together sounds to make a symphony that has never been heard before. Such creativity reflects more than a simple evolution of the mind. Even the atheist Sigmund Freud admitted, "The nature of artistic achievement is psychologically inaccessible to us."[6]

Dorothy Sayers states that our creative acts are an expression of the image and likeness of God within us.[7] We are given the ability to create because we are made in the image of the one who created the universe.

A third uniquely human characteristic is a sense of *morality*. All people have a "conscience," a sense of right and wrong within them. For example, anthropologists recognize that every culture has certain actions that are always considered wrong (i.e., incest, murder, stealing). These "crimes" may take different forms, pertaining to the culture, but a sense of "wrong" is always present. If this were not so, how could the United Nations unanimously condemn a nation for human rights violations?

From where does this sense of morality come? Biblically, it is one aspect of being created in the image of God that separates us from the animals. We have God's Law "written on our hearts" (Rom. 2:14-15), which makes us aware that we are moral beings who are answerable for our actions.

Our personality, creativity, and morality, are best explained by the existence of a personal, creative, and moral God in whose image we are created (Gen. 1:26-27; 5:1; James 3:9). The fascinating qualities of humanity reveal that we are God's work of art, fashioned to reflect His image.

The evidence for the existence of God as seen in the universe and humanity seems overwhelming. How can some people not see the hand of God in the awesome majesty of a starry night or the grandeur of the Rocky Mountains? How can anyone reject the existence of a loving and good God when they experience powerful emotions or a twinge of their conscience?

The Evidence Encourages Belief

God does not exist simply because I believe that He does. He has not left us guessing about His presence and concern for His creation. The evidence is strong and clear.

Can we "prove" that God exists? No, not in the scientific sense; no more than I could "prove" that I love my wife. I can, however, point to compelling evidence of my love for my wife which would make you conclude that my love for her *does* exist. In a similar way, we can point to the evidence for God and also conclude that He exists. This evidence reassures us until that great day when "our faith shall be sight."

Discussion Questions

1. Why do some people reject the existence of God? How do they explain away the evidence of His existence?

2. How would you answer the following remarks?
   a. "A good God would not allow disasters and disease and crime."
   b. "Man is so limited that there is no way he could ever know anything about God even if He *did* exist."

3. How does the universe point to the existence of God?

4. In spite of mankind's failings, we still bear the imprint of God's creative work. In what ways?

5. What does the Bible reveal about God that we would not otherwise know?

Further Reading

C. Stephen Evans, *The Quest for Faith* (Downers Grove, Ill.: InterVarsity Press, 1982).

Arthur F. Holmes, *Contours of a World View* (Grand Rapids: Wm. B. Eerdmans, 1983), chapters 8 and 9.

J.P. Moreland, *Scaling the Secular City: A Defense of Christianity* (Grand Rapids: Baker Book House, 1987).

R.C. Sproul, *Reason to Believe* (Grand Rapids: Zondervan Publishing House, 1978). See his discussion of the problem of evil, chapters 8 and 9.

Keith Yandell, *Christianity and Philosophy* (Grand Rapids: Wm. B. Eerdmans, 1984). See especially chapter 6: "Is the Existence of Evil Evidence against the Existence of God?"

CHAPTER FIVE

Why Believe in the Bible?

If we would destroy the Christian religion, we must first of all destroy man's belief in the Bible.
Voltaire

The reason people are down on the Bible is that they're not up on the Bible.
William Ward Ayer

Every word of God is flawless; He is a shield to those who take refuge in Him. Do not add to His words, or He will rebuke you and prove you a liar.
Proverbs 30:5-6, NIV

Rowland Hill, the fiery British preacher of the nineteenth century, once received a letter criticizing him for driving to church in his carriage. After all, the writer complained, the Bible never mentions carriages, and Jesus certainly never drove one to the temple.

Hill agreed and then added, "If the writer of this letter would come to my house saddled and bridled next Sunday, I will gladly follow our Lord's example."[1]

Unfortunately, not all differences over the Bible have been settled with such humor. Zealots have often used the Bible as a weapon in many ideological battlefields, furiously quoting verses to condemn or support an issue.

Others scoff at those who believe that an "old, dusty book" could have anything to say to our modern, progressive society. For example, Dr. Lawrence Young, a physician in Virginia, feels that he must help people "who are afflicted with believing." He encourages some of his patients not to attend church or read the Bible. These practices, he says, inflict guilt and are not beneficial to their health.

"The Bible utilizes the wisdom of 2,000 years ago," Young says. "It's not satisfactory today for what we need."[2]

Why do Christians still believe the Bible? Why not just trust reason or common sense rather than a book? Do Christians have good reasons for believing the Bible?

The Necessity for the Bible

In the last chapter we saw that God has made Himself known through all that He has made. In the universe around us and in our own soul, we clearly see the reality of God. This revelation of God is called *general revelation.* It is *general in content* in that it reveals basic facts about God: He is the Creator, He is omnipotent, He has a personality, etc.

It is also *general in audience.* Everyone can look up into the heavens and feel the awe of God's creation. Each one of us senses God's holiness when our conscience begs for attention and cleansing.

But is this all we get? What plans does God have for the universe He has made and the human beings He has fashioned? What about me? How do I fit into the scheme of God's creation? Does He laugh at our feeble attempts to understand ourselves and our world? Would He allow us to wander through life in a fog of despair, wondering why we are here and where we are going?

We need answers to these vitally important questions, but the answers are not found in the stars or in my conscience. God must speak more specifically. And God has spoken.

Christians believe that God's verbal revelation is the Bible. A written record is the most accurate and safest way to record God's message. Christians call the Bible God's *special revelation* because it refers to specific acts and teachings by God which show man the way of redemption.

In saying that the Bible is God's Word, however, a host of questions confront us:

1. How did we get the Bible? Is it just a collection of writings by religious men?

2. Is God's revelation found *only* in the Bible? Why not the Muslim's Koran, the Buddhist's Bhagavad Gita, or the Hindu's Vedas?

3. Why are *these* books in the Bible? Why were some books included and others left out?

4. You can make the Bible mean anything you want, can't you? Is there *one* meaning for what the Bible teaches?

These questions require a more complete response than is possible here, but this chapter will attempt to address some of the basic issues involved with each question.

How Did We Get the Bible?

The Bible is a book of dual authorship: God and man. We cannot say that the Bible is totally a product of man because that denies the overwhelming claim that it contains the very words of God. On the other hand, we cannot say that the Bible is totally a product of God. The human element is too clearly seen in the variety of writing styles. The process of God's revelation being recorded in the Bible is pictured on page 75. *Inspiration* is the process by which God supervises the human authors to accurately record His message. How does God do this? Here is the mystery. The Scriptures themselves are helpful at this point. Two well-known passages give us insight into the process.

The first is found in Paul's second letter to Timothy:

> All Scripture is inspired by God and profitable for teaching, for reproof, for correction, for training in righteousness; that the man of God may be adequate, equipped for every good work (2 Tim. 3:16-17).

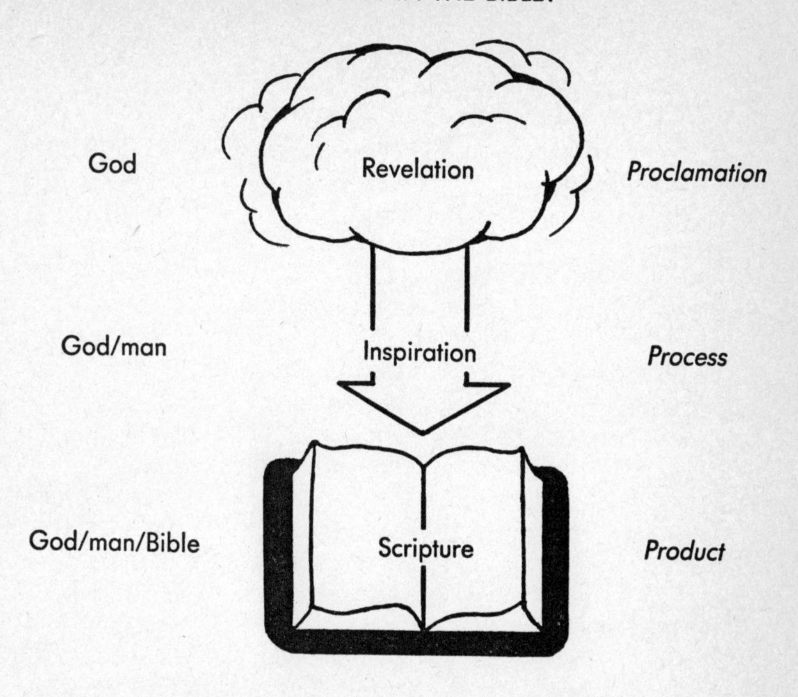

Fig. 3 From God to us: The recording of God's message

In this passage, the term *inspired* is an unusual term denoting "God's breath." The word refers to the breath of God as He speaks, implying that the Scriptures are to be understood as God's voice.

This passage also teaches that the Scriptures themselves are inspired, not the human authors. The human authors were certainly inspired (as we shall see in 2 Peter 1:20-21), but the absence of any mention of them in this verse is striking.

Finally, Paul does not make a distinction among the various writings contained in the Scriptures. He claims that "all Scripture" should be accepted as the breath of God.

A second passage, giving us some insight into the process of inspiration, is found in Peter's second letter:

> But know this first of all, that no prophecy of Scripture is a matter of one's own interpretation, for no prophecy was ever made by an act of human will, but men moved by the Holy Spirit spoke from God (2 Peter 1:20-21).

Several observations should be made from this passage. First, the word *prophecy* refers either to the prophetic message of the Old Testament or to the Old Testament as a whole. In either case, the prophecies came as a result of God's intentions to communicate, not man's desire to record "his religious feelings."

Second, the inspiration process is described as "men moved by the Holy Spirit." The Spirit did not simply use them as typewriters or overrule their personalities to speak; rather the entire person was "moved" by the Spirit. The term *moved* was often used to describe a ship carried along by the wind (see Acts 27:15, 17). British theologian Michael Green applies this meaning of the word to the passage in 2 Peter: "The prophets raised their sails, so to speak [they were obedient and receptive], and the Holy Spirit filled them and carried their craft along in the direction He wished."[3]

Finally, we must note that the men "spoke *from* God." They did not speak *about* God nor even speak *for* God. The source of their message is God Himself.

Without taking away the individual personalities and styles of the human authors, God supervised the recording of His message. This makes the Bible very human as well as very divine. Someone may say, "Well, then, the Bible must contain errors. After all, 'To err is human.' "

While it is true that no human is perfect, the adage "To err is human" does not mean that humans *must always* make mistakes. We are right some of the time, aren't we? God's role in inspiration kept the human authors from error as they accurately recorded His message.

Although the process of inspiration cannot be fully understood, one thing is certain: it is clearly taught in the Scriptures. The Bible unapologetically refers to itself as the Word of God. Over 3,800 times in the Old Testament alone we find the expression "Thus says the Lord" or a similar phrase. But is this so odd? If any writing really *is* God's message, we would expect it to say so.

Why Should We Trust the Bible?

Now that we have examined the inspiration of the Scriptures, we must also take note of what Jesus Himself has to say about the Scriptures.

As Christians, we believe in Jesus Christ; therefore, we must also believe His teaching about the Bible. We cannot say, "I'm a follower of Jesus, but I do not believe what He taught."

If Jesus were just another man giving His opinions, then we would be foolish to follow His teachings as though they were the truth. But Jesus claimed to be more than just "another teacher." He said, "For I did not speak on my own initiative, but the Father Himself who sent Me has given Me commandment, what to say, and what to speak. And I know that His commandment is eternal life; therefore the things I speak, I speak just as the Father has told Me" (John 12:49-50).

The divine teachings of Jesus reveal at least four major truths about the Bible. First, Jesus considered the Scriptures *the very words of God.* For example, He used the expression "For God said" to introduce quotations from the Old Testament (see Matt. 15:4, 22:31-32). While recognizing the human element in the Scriptures, He nevertheless asserted that what was recorded were the Words of God: "David himself said in the Holy Spirit" (Mark 12:36). This same understanding of inspiration is echoed by the Apostle Peter when he states that the Holy Spirit "spoke by the mouth of David" (Acts 1:16).

Second, because Jesus considered the Scriptures to be the very words of God, He also considered the Word of

God *authoritative.* Jesus constantly rebuked the religious leaders of His day by appealing to their misuse or neglect of the Scriptures: "And why do you yourselves transgress the commandment of God for the sake of your tradition?" (Matt. 15:3) He reprimanded the Jewish leaders for their ignorance of the Word of God (Mark 12:18-27).

Third, Jesus considered the Old Testament to be *historically accurate.* The events described in the Old Testament have been assailed by critics who doubt the historical accuracy of almost every narrative recorded. Thus, it is comforting to view Jesus' straightforward use of the people and events of the Old Testament. Almost 10 percent of Jesus' recorded conversations consists of direct quotations of the Old Testament.[4]

Here is a partial list of the people and events that Jesus referred to as historical:

Abel (Luke 11:51)
Noah (Matt. 24:37-39)
Lot (Luke 17:28-32)
The creation of man and woman (Matt. 19:4)
The Flood (Luke 17:27)
The destruction of Sodom and Gomorrah (Matt. 10:15)
The manna from heaven (John 6:31, 49, 58)
The healing of Namaan by Elisha (Luke 4:27)

Referring to Jesus' use of the Old Testament, John Wenham notes: "Curiously enough, the narratives that are least acceptable to the so-called 'modern mind' are the very ones that he seemed most fond of choosing for his illustrations."[5]

Finally, Jesus considered the Scriptures *unchangeable.* When He pronounced that "Scripture cannot be broken" (John 10:35), He meant that the Word of God cannot be annulled or denied. The Scriptures may be ignored and attacked, but they stand unbreakable and true.

What about the New Testament? Since it was composed

after Jesus departed from the earth, He could not have personally given His stamp of approval on the writings. But He did the next best thing. He clearly stated that future revelation was forthcoming and would be guided by the Holy Spirit (John 14:26).

Jesus Christ viewed the Scriptures as the authoritative revelation of God; therefore, we who follow Christ can be confident in trusting the Bible.

Why Are These Books in the Bible?

The advertisement was enticing: "The Lost Books of the Bible." The intriguing volume contained twenty or so writings "which had been suppressed by the church for centuries." These books had been hidden, it was claimed, because they contradicted what the church leaders wanted the people to believe. The stories contained in these writings gave further insight into the lives of Adam and Eve, filled in the "missing years" of the life of Christ, and unlocked other mysteries unexplained in the Bible—all for $3.95.

The "Lost Books of the Bible" are in reality ancient Jewish and Christian writings. Some of these books were written in the period between the Old and New Testaments (the Old Testament Apocrypha and Pseudepigrapha) while others were second- and third-century Christian works (the New Testament Apocrypha).

When we realize that there are such a large number of ancient writings, several questions immediately come to our minds: "Why does the Bible contain the books it does? What about these other books? Who made the decision to include some books and exclude others?"

When we ask the question "Why *these* books?" we are discussing the issue of canonicity. The canon—the list of books accepted to be a part of God's revelation—was determined separately for the Old Testament and the New Testament. Very little is written about the process, but what evidence we do have shows an amazing agreement among God's people as to what belonged in the Bible.

The Old Testament

Jesus often spoke of the inspiration and authority of "the Law" or "the Scriptures." What Scriptures was He talking about? His references point to the fact that a recognized body of writing was already accepted as the Bible.

One passage of Scripture which possibly indicates the extent of the Old Testament canon at the time of Jesus is Matthew 23:35. In this context, Jesus is indicting the religious leaders because of their killing of God's prophets "from the blood of righteous Abel to the blood of Zechariah, the son of Berechiah." Since Abel was killed in Genesis (4:8) and the murder of Zechariah is recorded in 2 Chronicles (24:20-22), Jesus seems to be saying "from the first book of the Bible to the last."

Indeed, the Hebrew Bible does begin with the Book of Genesis and end with the last historical book, 2 Chronicles. Though the arrangement is different, our current Old Testament contains the same books found in the Hebrew Scriptures.

Further evidence from other Jewish writers, such as Josephus (*Contra Apion* 1.8), points to this same conclusion. The Jewish teachers considered the canon of Scripture closed after the writings of the latter prophets. Sometime in the first century, a rabbi expressed the common Jewish belief: "With the death of Haggai, Zechariah and Malachi, the latter prophets, the Holy Spirit ceased out of Israel" (Tosephta Sota 13.2). The list of books in the Old Testament given by the Christian bishop Melito in A.D. 170 also agrees.

The Roman Catholic church includes a number of books in the Old Testament that are not found in the Protestant Bible. These writings, known as the *Apocrypha*, were composed after the completion of the last Hebrew Old Testament book and before the writing of the New Testament. These apocryphal books include: Tobit, Judith, Wisdom,

Sirach, Baruch, and 1 and 2 Maccabees.

These books officially became a part of the Catholic Bible in 1546 at the Council of Trent. This decision was made in response to the reformers claims that these books were not a part of God's scriptural revelation.[6] Because the Apocrypha was not included in the Bible which Jesus used and quoted, Protestants believe the books should not be added to the Old Testament. Protestants and Catholics do agree on the canon of the New Testament.

New Testament

In the first century, Christianity was illegal, and Christian writings were often confiscated and destroyed. In spite of these early difficulties, we have over 5,000 Greek manuscripts of the New Testament, copied secretly by believers. Add to this evidence the discovery of vast numbers of ancient translations and quotations by early writers and there is little room to doubt the authenticity of the New Testament.

But this still does not answer the question of how the books were accepted into the canon. Although many books were purported to be written by disciples of Christ, early Christians came to a general consensus as to which writings were the Word of God.

The underlying criteria for accepting a writing as the inspired Word of God was twofold: the writing must have *apostolic authority* and *church-wide acceptance. Apostolic authority* refers to the fact that each book of the New Testament was either written by or approved by one of the original apostles as the inspired Word of God. The early church was "built upon the foundation of the apostles and the prophets" (Eph. 2:20) and devoted to "the apostles' teaching and fellowship" (Acts 2:42). Jesus made a special promise that the Holy Spirit would guide the apostles in all truth (John 16:13) and bring all things to their remembrance (John 14:26).

Furthermore, each book of the New Testament received

acceptance from believers at large. Christians in the early church, from all walks of life, recognized the divine authority of the writings. God's sheep know His voice (John 10:14-16, 27).

When the Christian church became more organized, councils of church leaders formally acknowledged what books had been accepted as canonical. By A.D. 367, Athanasius, the bishop of Alexandria, recorded that the Christian New Testament consisted of the twenty-seven books we have now.[7]

If the sovereign God went to such lengths to reveal His word to humanity, would He not also supervise the recognition of these writings?

How Can We Understand the Bible?

Once we have established that the Bible is genuinely God's revelation to man, we still have the responsibility to correctly interpret what it says. Unfortunately, many people who believe that the Bible is God's Word treat it as though it were a lucky charm or a crystal ball.

Furthermore, the abuses of Bible interpretation are legion. As Shakespeare wrote in *The Merchant of Venice*, "The devil can cite Scripture for his purpose." From many pulpits in Nazi Germany, the Bible was quoted as support for the nation's violence against the Jews. Such misuse of the Bible should be a constant reminder that we cannot make the Bible mean whatever we want it to mean.

The guiding principle in biblical interpretation must be seeking to understand what the original authors (human and Divine) intended a certain passage to mean. The following three guidelines for interpretation of the Bible are helpful.

1. *We must understand that the Bible is literature* While this sounds simplistic, this concept remains at the heart of biblical study. Since God revealed His Word in letters, stories, and poems, His meaning is understood in light of these literary forms. Determining the correct mean-

ing of an isolated verse is almost impossible if we fail to see it as a single thread in the literary fabric woven by the author. *Poetic language* ("The trees clap their hands" Isa. 55:12) and other *figures of speech* ("I am the door" John 10:9) must be interpreted in the Bible just as they would be interpreted in any lyrical composition.

2. *We must understand the differences between biblical times and modern times.* Our society is a Western, technological system. The Bible came to an ancient, Near-Eastern/Greco-Roman culture that was essentially agrarian. These societal changes do not diminish the message of Scripture, but they do remind us that we view God's Word through a different framework. Good Bible encyclopedias and dictionaries are invaluable in bridging the gap between biblical times and today.

3. *We must recognize that the Bible was progressively revealed.* God revealed His Word over a period of 1,500 years. Over that span of time God unveiled, step by step, His purpose and program for the redemption of humanity. What God revealed to His people at the beginning served as the groundwork for what He would reveal later. The New Testament does not nullify the meaning of the Old Testament; rather it completes what God began. The coming of Jesus marked a new step in God's plan (Heb. 1:1-2). The Old Testament is valuable to us today "for our instruction" (Rom. 15:4), yet the requirements of God's Law were fulfilled in the death and resurrection of Christ (Rom. 3:25-26; Heb. 9:11–10:18). Without this understanding of progressive revelation, we would be bound to a confusing system of Sabbath sacrifices, Sunday worship, and dietary laws—all under the authority of "literal interpretation."

Putting the Bible in Perspective

The Bible is neither a "paper pope" nor an instrument to be wielded as a weapon in the hands of man. It is the living and dynamic revelation of God Himself to be read, studied, experienced, and obeyed.

The Bible is not a book to be worshiped; it has authority only because it is the breath of God. It is like a phonograph record containing the voice of God. The record itself has value only because of the "Recording Artist."[8] The Word of God is intended to lead us to the God of the Word. In it He has given us the words of eternal life. John Wesley summed it up best:

> I want to know one thing—the way to heaven; how to land on that happy shore. God Himself has condescended to teach the way: for this very end He came from heaven. He hath written it down in a book. Oh, give me that book! At any price give me the book of God![9]

Discussion Questions

1. Why is the special revelation of the Bible necessary?
2. Describe the difference between "revelation" and "inspiration."
3. What two key passages of Scripture give a biblical perspective on inspiration? What do these passages tell us?
4. A modern writer stated: "The Bible nowhere claims to be the words of God." How would you answer him?
5. What was Jesus' view of the Bible?
6. How do the Protestant and Roman Catholic Bibles differ?
7. What examples of the Bible being misused have you heard?

Further Reading

Norman L. Geisler and William E. Nix, *A General Introduction to the Bible* (Chicago: Moody Press, 1968).

Kenneth Barker, gen. ed., *NIV Study Bible* (Grand Rapids: Zondervan Bible Publishers, 1985).

R.C. Sproul, *Knowing Scripture* (Downers Grove, Ill.: InterVarsity Press, 1977).

T. Norton Sterrett, *How to Understand Your Bible* (Downers Grove, Ill.: InterVarsity Press, 1974).

CHAPTER SIX

Why Believe in Jesus?

Gentlemen, it would be easy to start a new religion to compete with Christianity. All the founder would have to do is die and then be raised from the dead.

Voltaire

I founded my empire upon what?—force. Jesus founded His empire on love: and at this hour millions would die for him.

Napoleon Bonaparte

Not long ago I was teaching a college extension class in a state penitentiary. Some of the students were Christians, but the majority were not. This was not a class to promote religious views but rather a class to examine the backgrounds and early history of Christianity.

The men were fascinated with our exploration into the history and literature of the first century. But whenever the topic of our discussion turned to the person of Jesus Christ, the men expressed strong feelings.

One fellow in particular became very animated when he gave his views on Jesus. "Jesus could not have risen from the dead," he proclaimed loudly one evening. "There's no way."

Trying to foster more discussion, I asked, "Why not?"

"Because that would mean He was God," he replied. "And that just can't be true."

"But that's what the Bible says happened," one of the other inmates interjected.

"I don't care what the Bible says. It didn't happen . . . and there's no way you or anybody else can prove it."

He slammed his book shut and stared at the table. Several weeks later he dropped the class because talking about Jesus "bothered him."

What bothered him was not that anyone was preaching about Jesus; that was forbidden by the nature of the class. It was the person of Jesus Christ that irritated him. Talking about the church and biblical literature was fine, but he felt that the words and works of Jesus demanded some response on his part. He chose to reject Him.

This man's struggle with the person of Christ was the result of a knowledgeable understanding of the claims of Christ. He recognized that Christianity was unique because of who Jesus is. Christianity **IS** Christ.

Who Is Jesus?

In His own time Jesus profoundly influenced social and religious systems. He was not a boring theologian but a storyteller who gathered a following that ranged from the curious to the committed. Although His teachings focused on knowing God, He was accused of not being religious enough. He asked unsettling questions, went to parties with people of reproachable character, healed the sick, raised the dead, and publicly condemned a religious system that plotted to assassinate Him.

Jesus was a real person. Like every other person, Jesus was born, grew up, and died. He had a human body, human desires, and human thoughts. He possessed normal human features (John 2:21) and a human soul (Matt. 26:38). He shared in all of our human weaknesses and limitations. He became hungry (Matt. 4:2), thirsty (John 19:28), tired (John 4:6), and sleepy (Matt. 8:24). He experienced the full range of human emotions: sorrow (Matt. 26:37), anger (Mark 3:5), joy (Luke 10:21), and love (John 11:34-36).

In only one area was He immune to human frailty; He was not marred by the effects of sin: "And in Him is no sin" (1 John 3:5). Jesus was tempted to sin (Matt. 4:1-11), but because of His divine nature He never yielded (Heb. 4:15).

Jesus was a genuine human being. But we cannot stop

there. He was not just one of us; He claimed to be much more. He claimed to be God-incarnate, not just God's representative but God Himself.

This concept is not acceptable to the "modern" mind. Many people argue that a transcendent God would not, and could not, become a man. Even some of those who do believe in God regard the claim that Jesus is God as a logical impossibility. How could an infinite God be located in a finite human body? Many skeptics feel that whatever Jesus accomplished by His teachings and sacrifice could have been performed by any man. Thus, the deity of Jesus Christ is an unnecessary invention of His early followers who sought to deify Him after His death, much as the followers of Buddha deified their god.

Contemporary Views of Jesus

In the summer of 1988, Hollywood director Martin Scorsese released *The Last Temptation of Christ*, a movie which portrayed a befuddled Jesus who knows neither His identity nor His mission. The film, based on the 1955 novel by Nikos Kazantzakis, presents a portrait of Christ which denies the biblical account of His life and ministry. Scorsese claims to be unconvinced by the Bible and prefers a Jesus who calls Himself a hypocrite and who fantasizes about committing adultery.

Kazantzakis and Scorsese are not alone in their attempts to fabricate a Jesus apart from the Bible. Skeptics have often claimed that the Bible does not give an accurate account of the life of Jesus. Under the guise of scholarly study, the person of Jesus is reduced to an individual who barely resembles the Jesus of the Scriptures. Much of the biblical record of the life of Christ is jettisoned in an attempt to focus on a contemporary Jesus, a "Jesus who relates to me and my world."

From historical scholarship to the Hollywood screen, Jesus is recast to fit the whims of modern imaginations. Let's examine some of these contemporary views of Jesus.

1. **Jesus, The "Good" Man.** Today most people agree that Jesus was a man who lived an exemplary life of kindness and integrity. His humble desire to help others was the motivation of His ministry. He cared for the bereaved, encouraged the outcasts and gave hope to the oppressed.

He taught His followers to love one another, and He challenged the religious leaders of His day to demonstrate their faith by humanitarian acts.

But many modern thinkers claim that Jesus was *only* a good man, nothing more—not God, not even a prophet. His fame rests in the fact that He was posthumously raised to the status of God by His starry-eyed followers. It is believed that the Virgin Birth of Jesus, His miracles, and His resurrection were myths invented after Christ's death to bolster the claim that Jesus was God-incarnate. The historical Jesus was no more unique than any other teacher of "sacred truth." The records of the Gospels, these thinkers claim, are filled with fanciful tales which in no way give us any truth about the historical Jesus.

The only value of Jesus for modern man, say the proponents of this view, is that Jesus gives us the classic example of sacrificial love. But since our knowledge of Jesus is rooted in such a jaded record (the New Testament), Christianity would be better off to erase the memory of Jesus completely and look to others as examples of proper living. Theologian and author Deane Ferm suggests Martin Luther King or Martin Buber as more contemporary examples to follow.[1] Others suggest Gandhi, Albert Schweitzer, or Mother Teresa.

This is truly Christianity without Christ. If Christ is not uniquely the Son of God, then His teachings are on the same level as other "good" men of history. The teachings concerning His purpose and work are rejected. All that is left is "do good unto others," a reflection of modern, works-oriented religion that makes the death of Christ a meaningless event (Gal. 2:21). This is fashionable teaching for our world today but hardly the life-changing spiritual message of the Gospel that turned the world upside down.

2. **Jesus, The "Very Religious" Man.** Another approach is to see Jesus Christ as a *man* who was so *close* to God that we can learn about God through His life. Dutch theologian Ellen Flesseman summarizes this approach: "The Son Jesus Christ is not God, but a man who was so one with God that in Him I meet God."[2]

Jesus as the "very religious man" differs only slightly from the view of Jesus as a "good" man. As we shall see later in this chapter, Jesus claimed to be more than a *way* to God; He claimed to be *God Himself.*

Those who hold this view believe that if we want God to be profoundly present with us, we just need to see how Jesus did it and follow His example.

But this immediately presents a problem. Must I pick and choose among the recorded teachings of Jesus, find what I like, and follow those teachings? Must I attack religious institutions, speak authoritatively from God, allow myself to be wrongly accused, and suffer execution without uttering a word in my defense? If I am only to follow the moral imperatives of Jesus (which is a very small percentage of His teaching), then why do I need Jesus at all?

3. **Jesus, the "Chosen" Man.** Another contemporary view of Jesus is that He is *functionally* divine but *essentially* merely a man. In his book, *The Human Face of God,* John A.T. Robinson, an Anglican clergyman, states that Jesus is not a divine or semidivine being who comes from the other side. He is a human raised up from among his brethren to be the instrument of God's decisive work.[3] In other words, Jesus was a man handpicked by God to show His love to mankind. God could have chosen anyone, but Jesus got the nod. As a result, says Robinson, we are wasting our time talking about *who* Jesus is—He is one of us! The importance of Jesus is found in what God did through Him.

While it is true that Jesus was "the instrument of God's decisive work," His work was only effective because of *who* He is—God-incarnate. Before we can experience the benefits of what Jesus has done, we must first believe correctly about who He is (John 8:24).

4. **Jesus, the "Revolutionary" Man**. In many Third World countries the poor and oppressed people place their hope in revolution. They often read the Bible as a source of revolutionary teachings. Did not Jesus teach that the poor should be given priority in the kingdom? Did not Jesus Himself stand against the oppressive leaders of His day and reveal their wickedness? Did not Jesus promise to bring a sword in His battle against the rulers of this world?

Those who believe that Jesus promotes revolution reduce all of the teachings of Jesus and the New Testament to whatever applies to liberation for the huddled masses, the politically oppressed, or whatever minority chooses to revolt. The various expressions of "liberation theology" are best described as Marxism dressed in the vernacular of the Bible.

Jesus certainly taught that every believer has a responsibility to alleviate poverty and suffering, but helping others should be the result of having faith in Christ, not seeking for political gain. The Gospel message speaks of a spiritual revolution, not a political one. While we must recognize that the Gospel has profound social and political implications, we cannot dilute Jesus' priority of seeking and saving the lost (Luke 19:10).

5. **Jesus, The "New Age" Man**. The New Age movement, a potpourri of modern pantheism and positive thinking (see chapter 3), suggests that Jesus was just one among many "christs" or "enlightened masters" who have appeared on the earth to bestow divine teaching to the world. While Jesus was in some way "divine," He was not unique in this function. There were many "christs" before Him,

and there have been many since

New Agers believe that a New Age christ is coming who will bring with him the Age of Aquarius, a new era of peace and prosperity for the world. Jesus Christ is honored because of His contribution to our overall understanding of the coming New Age, but the proponents of the New Age gospel quickly explain that He cannot be the unique, divine revelation of God because we are all God.

Here we see a good example of a religion trying desperately to work Jesus into its teachings. The historical Jesus just doesn't fit with New Age doctrine, so a New Age christ is manufactured to fill the bill. Missing from the New Age picture of Christ are the biblical claims that He is the *only* way to the Father (John 14:6; Acts 4:12) and the sovereign Lord of all things (Phil. 2:10-11; 1 Peter 4:11).

What Are We to Think?

All of these approaches to the person of Jesus Christ have enough truth to make them acceptable—to a point. They all attempt to make Jesus more "real" to the present-day situation. First, these approaches make the person of Jesus easily understood by the modern mind. They have taken the mystery away; He was only one of us doing a wonderful work. Second, these approaches clothe Jesus in modern garb, making Him concerned about contemporary issues.

Is it really wise to claim that Jesus Christ is uniquely God-incarnate? Shouldn't we be open-minded and allow an array of mixed views and reviews about the person of Jesus Christ?

Jesus Himself would not be pleased with such an approach. He once asked His disciples, "Who do people say that the Son of Man is?" (Matt. 16:13) They responded with a number of the most popular views: John the Baptist reincarnated, Elijah, or one of the other prophets returned (Matt. 16:14).

Jesus then asked the blunt question, "Who do you say that I am?" (Matt. 16:15) Jesus seemed to be saying, "Lay aside the popular opinions about Me. Who do YOU think I am?" This is the vital question that continues to confront mankind.

The Apostle Peter responded to Jesus by proclaiming, "Thou art the Christ, the Son of the living God" (Matt. 16:16). Jesus commended Peter's confession: "Blessed are you, Simon Barjona, because flesh and blood did not reveal this to you, but my Father who is in heaven" (Matt. 16:17).

Unlike other religions which emphasize the acceptance of certain rules of conduct, Christianity begins and ends with one's acceptance of and devotion to the person of Jesus Christ. The invitation "Follow Me" (Luke 9:59) is the heart of Christian faith. It involves an acknowledgement of who Christ is and a commitment to follow His teachings.

Can We Believe That Jesus Christ Is God?

Can a case be made for supporting that Jesus Christ the man was truly God? Notice that the question is not: Can we *understand* that Jesus Christ is God? but: Is there good reason to *believe* that He is God?

Based on the record of Scripture, the answer is an unqualified yes. Two major lines of evidence within Scripture lead us to this conclusion. First, Jesus' claims to deity, and His miracles and resurrection, overwhelmingly attest to His divine nature. Second, New Testament authors refer to the deity of Jesus Christ as a fundamental truth.

Evidence from the Life and Teachings of Jesus

Those who deny the deity of Jesus usually claim that the Gospel writers put words in the mouth of Jesus regarding His deity. In the New Testament accounts of the life of Jesus, however, we find many explicit as well as implicit claims that Jesus is genuinely God.

Jesus forgave sins. Forgiving sins is a prerogative reserved for God alone, yet Jesus clearly takes that privilege for Himself (Mark 2:1-12). C.S. Lewis makes much of this activity of Jesus. How could Jesus forgive offenses against

God unless He was God Himself? I cannot forgive another person unless that person has offended me. In fact, to forgive someone is my way of acknowledging that I have been offended. Thus, for Jesus to forgive sins committed against God is a bold declaration of His deity.[4]

Jesus promised to return and judge the world. In the Old Testament, the final judgment was an eschatological event performed by God (Dan. 12:1-2; Mal. 3:5). Jesus unequivocally takes on Himself this role and even uses the passages from the Old Testament to describe His participation in the future judgment (Matt. 25:31; 26:63-65; John 5:27).

Jesus refers to the angels who will accompany Him at this time alternately as "God's angels" (Matt. 22:30) and "the Son of man's angels" (Matt. 13:41), a subtle, yet profound acknowledgement of His equality with God.

Jesus claimed identity with God the Father. The most explicit claims by Jesus of His deity are seen in John's Gospel. Here we find that Jesus admits that He existed with the Father before the world was created: "And now, glorify Thou Me together with Thyself, Father, with the glory which I had with Thee before the world was" (John 17:5). To the hostile Jewish leaders He stated that He had existed before Abraham (John 8:58).

Jesus further told His disciples, "He who has seen Me has seen the Father" (John 14:9) and acknowledged, "I and the Father are one" (John 10:30). His claims were noticed and misunderstood by the Jewish leaders who accused Him of blasphemy: "You, a mere man, claim to be God" (John 10:33, NIV; see also John 5:18, 19:7).

To say that Jesus never claimed to be God is to seriously misrepresent the biblical account of His life and teachings.

Jesus demonstrated His divine authority over the natural world by His miracles. According to the Gospel records, Jesus performed over thirty miracles. John reminds us that much of what Jesus did went unrecorded (John 21:25), so no doubt Jesus effected many miracles that were undocumented.

Each of the four Gospels gives accounts of many miraculous events in the life of Jesus. These events represent supernatural incursions of divine power which were clearly at the disposal of Jesus. His miracles ranged from a demonstration of His power over disease (Matt. 8:2-4) and blindness (John 9:1-7) to demons (Mark 1:23-26) and storms (Luke 8:22-25). His most decisive miracles reveal His authority over death itself. Three different individuals, after untimely deaths, were brought back to life by Jesus: Jairus' daughter (Mark 5:22-43); the widow's son (Luke 7:11-15); and Lazarus (John 11:1-44).

The miracles of Jesus were not just for show They pointed to a truth beyond the events: Jesus Christ was God. In the Gospel of John the miracles of Jesus are called "signs" (John 2:23), highlighting their significant role as indicators of the true nature of Christ.

The Grand Miracle: The Resurrection of Jesus. Of all the miracles associated with the life of Jesus Christ, one miracle stands above the rest. The resurrection of Jesus Christ from the dead is forever the distinguishing mark of Christianity. No other religion had such a beginning.

It is easy to see why the resurrection of Jesus Christ is rejected by many skeptics. To admit that Jesus actually rose from the dead is to affirm all that He said and did as recorded in the Gospels. In fact, Paul emphatically announced that Jesus was "declared with power to be the Son of God by His resurrection from the dead" (Rom. 1:4, NIV).

Three strands of evidence point to the reality of Christ's resurrection: the empty tomb, the post-resurrection appearances of Christ, and the origin of the Christian church.

To publicly proclaim that Jesus had been raised from the dead while His body remained inside a sealed tomb would have been the height of folly. Surely the Jewish leaders would have produced the body of Jesus and exposed the whole affair as a farce. But they never did. The tomb was empty.

A second strand of evidence supporting the resurrection of Christ is the record of at least ten separate appearances of Christ after His death and burial which are presented by the biblical writers as straightforward fact. They did not make light of the event; instead they were careful to indicate the effort Christ took to prove His resurrection: "To [the apostles] He also presented Himself alive, after His suffering, *by many convincing proofs*, appearing to them over a period of forty days" (Acts 1:3, emphasis added). One writer even noted that some doubted and were not ready to accept that the Resurrection had occurred (Matt. 28:17). The post-resurrection appearances of Christ were not limited to a few emotional followers a short time after Christ's execution. Jesus appeared to many, including 500 at one time (1 Cor. 15:6), over a period of forty days.

This leads us to the final strand of evidence supporting the truth of Christ's resurrection: the beginning of the church. After the crucifixion of Christ, the disciples were in no shape to give their lives so completely to what appeared to be a failed cause; so how do we explain the inception of a movement with such a vast impact on an antagonistic culture except by the means of a cataclysmic miracle?

That the disciples considered the Resurrection the focal point of the Gospel message is clear from the early preaching of the church. Paul summarized his Gospel as: "Christ died for our sins according to the Scriptures, and that He was buried, and that He was raised on the third day according to the Scriptures" (1 Cor. 15:3-4).

References to the historical Resurrection permeate Christian faith and practice. Easter is the highest holy day of the Christian year. Christians made Sunday their day of worship to commemorate Christ's resurrection on the first day of the week.

The disciples pinned every aspect of their faith on this one event. Paul gave up everything "that I may know Him, and the power of His resurrection and the fellowship of His sufferings, being conformed to His death; in order that I may attain to the resurrection from the dead" (Phil. 3:10-11).

The resurrection of Jesus is the one event that has forever sealed the hope of all who come to Christ.

Support from the Teachings of the Biblical Writers

Jesus' own claims to deity are corroborated by the teachings of His followers in the other writings of the New Testament.

First, *Jesus is called "God."* At least eight times in the New Testament, the writers distinctly ascribe the name *God* to Jesus Christ. In Romans 9:5, NIV, Paul refers to Christ as the one "who is God over all." He later reminds Titus that as Christians we are "looking for the blessed hope and the appearing of the glory of our great God and Saviour, Christ Jesus" (Titus 2:13). Similar expressions are also found in Hebrews 1:8; John 1:1-2; 1:18; 20:28; 2 Peter 1:1; and Acts 20:28.

Second, New Testament authors state that *Jesus possessed the attributes of God:* He was preexistent with the Father (Phil. 2:5-6); He sustains the universe (Col. 1:17); He is unchanging (Heb. 13:8); and He receives worship from angels (Heb. 1:6), men (Matt. 14:33), and all creation (Phil. 2:10).

Third, a powerful statement of Jesus' deity is that *He is called the Creator* (John 1:3; Col. 1:16; Heb. 1:12). The Bible claims that God *alone* is the Creator of the world: "Thus says the Lord, your Redeemer, and the one who formed you from the womb, *I, the Lord,* am the maker of all things, stretching out the heavens *Myself,* and spreading out the earth *all alone*" (Isa. 44:24, emphasis added). For the followers of Jesus to refer to Him as the "maker of all things" was a bold statement of His identification as the Creator God.

Fourth, biblical writers describe Jesus as *God in the flesh:* "Have this attitude in yourselves which was also in Christ Jesus, who, although He existed in the form of God, did not regard equality with God a thing to be grasped, but emptied Himself, taking the form of a bond-servant, and being made in the likeness of men" (Phil. 2:5-7). Paul's well-defined statement, "For in Him all the fulness of Deity dwells in bodily form" (Col. 2:9), is unambiguous in its affirmation of the true and full deity of Jesus Christ.

Jesus was not a man who became a god, but God who became a man. The mystery of this event is pondered by His followers but never denied.

In the New Testament, we are not confronted with obscure passages and innuendos about Jesus but with lively and undisguised declarations of His full humanity and deity. To ignore the evidence is not merely to reinterpret Scripture but to completely deny what the Bible affirms about Jesus Christ.

Jesus: the Bridge between Man and God

The fact of the Incarnation is the heart of the Christian message. The awesome truth that Jesus was fully God while He was fully man goes beyond our imagination, but the Bible is clear that both are true.

What does this mean? It means that when we want to know what God is like, we need only to look at Jesus. The sovereign Creator is not just "out there." He is also "right here." In Christ we see firsthand the compassion of God, the love of God, and the power of God. Jesus is truly Immanuel, "God with us."

The fact that the person of Jesus Christ revealed God to us sets the stage for the ultimate reason He came to earth: He came to die. Although He was full deity in eternity past, He became a man that He might bear "our sins in His body on the cross" (1 Peter 2:24). His sacrifice was "once for all" (Heb. 7:27): *one* death for *all* sin for *all* men for *all* time.

Because Jesus was both God *and* man, He completely bridged the gap between man and God. "Since then the children share in flesh and blood, He Himself likewise also partook of the same, that through death He might render powerless him who had the power of death, that is, the devil; and might deliver those who through fear of death were subject to slavery all their lives" (Heb. 2:14-15).

Too many modern critics have said, "We don't like Jesus as He appears in the Bible. Let's make Him like one of us—someone we can really love." The Bible does not leave this option open.

Our salvation comes through the God-Man, not some manufactured caricature of a wild-eyed revolutionary or a New Age mystic. The essential Jesus is fully God and fully man. The bridge from God to man is anchored solidly on both sides. He is the Creator, the Redeemer, and the Returning King. Anything less is not Jesus.

Discussion Questions

1. Why do so many people want a more contemporary "Jesus for me"?

2. Describe the various ways the life and ministry of Jesus have been reinterpreted to fit modern society.

3. Why is one's understanding of the person of Jesus Christ the focal point of faith?

4. In what ways does "the person of Jesus Christ rip a hole in history that secular historians cannot repair"?

5. How is the full deity of Jesus Christ supported from the Scriptures?

6. Discuss why it was necessary for God to become man.

Further Reading

F.F. Bruce, *Jesus: Lord and Savior* (Downers Grove, Ill.: InterVarsity Press, 1986).

Jon A. Buell and O. Quentin Hyder, *Jesus: God, Ghost or Guru?* (Grand Rapids: Zondervan Publishing House, 1978).

R.T. France, *The Evidence for Jesus* (Downers Grove, Ill.: InterVarsity Press, 1986).

I. Howard Marshall, *I Believe in the Historical Jesus* (Grand Rapids: Wm. B. Eerdmans, 1977).

J.P. Moreland, *Scaling the Secular City: A Defense of Christianity* (Grand Rapids: Baker Book House, 1987). See especially chapter 6: "The Resurrection of Jesus."

CHAPTER SEVEN

Why Believe in the Holy Spirit?

Holy Spirit, Truth Divine,
Dawn upon this soul of mine;
Word of God, and inward light,
Wake my spirit, clear my sight.
Samuel Longfellow

I should as soon attempt to raise flowers if there were no atmosphere, or produce fruits if there were neither light nor heat, as to regenerate man if I did not believe there was a Holy Ghost.
Henry Ward Beecher

We have not even heard whether there is a Holy Spirit.
Acts 19:2

"The Holy Spirit is a power or influence like the force in Star Wars."

"Oh," I responded. "So you don't believe that the Holy Spirit is God?"

"Oh no, of course not." He tucked his *Watchtower* magazine under his arm. "The Holy Spirit is only the influence of God, like the heat from the sun. The heat is not the sun but it comes from the sun."

****

"The Holy Spirit is more important than Jesus. Jesus ministered during His lifetime only, but since Pentecost, the age of the Holy Spirit is here."

Puzzled, I asked, "Have you ever trusted Christ as your personal Saviour?"

"That's not important," she replied. "The Holy Spirit is now the source of power and joy. Pray to Him, seek Him."

*****

Sixteen-year-old Scott was having problems with his guilty conscience. His pastor explained to him that Scott could rely on the Holy Spirit to guide and convict him. Scott sat thoughtfully for a moment and then asked innocently, "Who is the Holy Spirit?"

*****

Who Is the Holy Spirit?

Scott has raised an important question. Most of what we know about the Holy Spirit is learned implicitly from the Scriptures. Very few passages actually describe the nature and character of the Holy Spirit. With the exception of the few passages in John 14–16, we usually learn about the Holy Spirit by observing what He does. We discover that the Holy Spirit is *both* a person and God.

The Person of the Holy Spirit

The Bible describes the Holy Spirit as a *person*, not an impersonal force or influence. Because the word for "spirit" (*pneuma*) is a neuter term, we would expect pronouns referring to the Holy Spirit to be neuter or impersonal. But the Spirit is referred to as "He," not "it" or "that" (see John 16:13-14).

Furthermore, the Bible describes the Holy Spirit as a person with an intelligent mind (Acts 15:28; 1 Cor. 2:10), a will (1 Cor. 12:11), and emotions (Eph. 4:30). To call the Holy Spirit an "it" is to misunderstand completely the biblical picture.

Someone may say, "Wait a minute! A person has arms

and legs and loves and laughs. How can a 'spirit' also be a person?" The mistake in this reasoning is obvious: personality is not limited to a human body or human emotions. In fact, if anything, humans express limited personality while God alone possesses personality in its fullness. We have limited abilities to reason and perceive (1 Cor. 13:12), and the essential features of our personalities (mind, will, and emotions) have been diminished by sin (Rom. 7:14-24; Eph. 4:17-19). We must be careful not to demand that God meet our criteria for personhood. As God says through the psalmist, "You thought that I was just like you" (Ps. 50:21).

Once we have concluded that the Holy Spirit is a person, we are forced to consider another problem: Is the Holy Spirit a person separate from God the Father?

The early church struggled with this question about the relationship between the Father and the Holy Spirit. Originally, an early statement of the Christian faith, the Nicene Creed (A.D. 325), contained the simple affirmation, "I believe in the Holy Spirit." Soon the church was confronted with the Pneumatomacheans, a group of people who sought to do away with the belief in the Holy Spirit as a separate yet equal member of the Godhead. As a result, the Council of Constantinople in A.D. 381 added the following statement to the Nicene Creed: "And I believe in the Holy Spirit, the Lord and giver of life, who with the Father and Son together is worshiped and glorified, who spoke by the prophets."

The biblical record also presents the Holy Spirit as a separate person from the Father and the Son. Jesus called the Spirit "another comforter" (John 14:16) who would have a ministry *after* Christ had departed from the earth.

We will discuss the relationship of the Father, Son, and the Holy Spirit more fully in the next chapter.

The Deity of the Holy Spirit

The deity of the Holy Spirit is not stated explicitly in Scripture, but biblical evidence drives us to this conclusion.

First, the Holy Spirit demonstrates certain attributes which are reserved for God alone: omniscience (1 Cor. 2:10-11), eternality (Heb. 9:14), and omnipresence (Ps. 139:7-10). He was active at the Creation (Gen. 1:2) and is a source of God's power (Luke 1:35) and love (Rom. 15:30).

Second, parallel phrases reveal that the Spirit is to be equated with God. For example, the Bible states that we are "a temple of God" (1 Cor. 3:16-17) as well as "a temple of the Holy Spirit" (1 Cor. 6:19-20). Acts 5:3-4 includes parallel phrases about lying to the Holy Spirit and lying to God. Several other passages interchange the name of the Holy Spirit with the name of God. (Compare Isaiah 6:8-10 with Acts 28:25-27, and Exodus 17:2-7 with Hebrews 3:7-9.)

The third and most important biblical evidence supporting the deity of the Holy Spirit is the equal footing which the Holy Spirit shares with God the Father and Jesus Christ. For example, Christian baptism is said to be "in the name of the Father, Son, and the Holy Spirit" (Matt. 28:18-20). Paul's benediction at the end of his Second Letter to the Corinthians also confirms this equal identity: "The grace of our Lord Jesus Christ, and the love of God, and the fellowship of the Holy Spirit, be with you all" (2 Cor. 13:14). Paul has no hesitation saying, "Now the Lord is the Spirit" (2 Cor. 3:17).

With the biblical writers, we may confidently affirm that the Holy Spirit is fully God.

What Does the Holy Spirit Do?

The Father is presented in Scripture as the Sovereign Ruler, the Omniscient God, and the Omnipotent Lord. Jesus, the Son, is the Revealer, the Redeemer, and the Messiah.

When we think of the Holy Spirit, we think of a dove or tongues of fire, not the awesome portraits of incomprehensible deity which describe the Father and the Son. Why? It seems that the Holy Spirit is the one who is working in us and through us rather than right in front of us. His work is best described as relating God to man on a personal plane.

Three words sum up the Spirit's work on behalf of man: inward, upward, and outward.

The Inward Work of the Holy Spirit

J.B. Phillips noted, "Every time we say, 'I believe in the Holy Spirit,' we mean that there is a living God able and willing to enter human personality and change it."[1]

The most basic role of the Holy Spirit is to make sinful humanity aware of the existence and presence of God, convince us of our alienation from God, and lead us to Regeneration. Because of sin, each person has the ability to ignore the reality of God, to spurn the evidence of His presence. We can study the heavens or puzzle over the origin of our consciences and still not come to the realization that these point to the existence of God.

The Holy Spirit uses this evidence not only to reveal the nature of God (Rom. 1:20) but also to exhibit our alienation from Him. Jesus succinctly describes this ministry of the Spirit:

> But I tell you the truth, it is to your advantage that I go away; for if I do not go away, the Helper shall not come to you; but if I go, I will send Him to you. And He, when He comes, will convict the world concerning sin, and righteousness, and judgment: concerning sin, because they do not believe in Me; and concerning righteousness, because I go to the Father, and you no longer behold Me; and concerning judgment, because the ruler of this world has been judged (John 16:7-11).

The word *convict* may be better understood as "convince." The Holy Spirit convinces the world of *sin*—that each person is imperfect and falls short of God's standard. That standard is *righteousness*, seen in the life of Jesus Christ. Because of the disparity between man's sinfulness and God's righteousness, the Holy Spirit further convinces man that there is a price to pay, a *judgment* to endure.

By revealing man's need, the Spirit sets the stage for His most dynamic work: regeneration. When man responds to the convicting work of the Spirit and becomes aware of God's loving provision to meet his need through the death of Christ, he stands ready to enter into God's family through faith. Then the Holy Spirit enters the life of the believer and changes him. He becomes a "new creature; the old things passed away; behold, new things have come" (2 Cor. 5:17).

Paul calls this the "renewing by the Holy Spirit" (Titus 3:5). This renewal is the beginning of the Holy Spirit's continuing presence in the life of the believer. Jesus promised this indwelling would characterize His followers after His departure (John 14:17).

Rather than having an external law to follow, Christians are said to have an internal guide and encourager. Each believer is responsible to heed the leading of the Holy Spirit in order to overcome sinful temptations: "But I say, walk by the Spirit, and you will not carry out the desire of the flesh" (Gal. 5:16).

The point of the inward work of the Holy Spirit is that God has not left us on our own to fend for ourselves Rather, God Himself, in the Person of the Holy Spirit, dwells within us to comfort, convict, encourage, and guide His children. The Holy Spirit is the "seal" of ownership that God places on His children (Eph. 4:30).

The Upward Work of the Holy Spirit

My wife and I spent several months traveling and teaching in Eastern Europe. The most frustrating aspect of our time there was our inability to speak the language and understand the culture. We could not develop close relationships. We could not even carry on a conversation.

We picked up the meanings of a few words and could slightly comprehend certain road signs, but we were forced to rely on our little book of "phrases used most often" to find a rest room or order something recognizable to eat.

There we were, immersed in a culture, yet feeling very much like outsiders.

It wasn't until we joined up with a translator that we began to understand what was going on around us. She made the whole country come alive to us. Now we could talk to anyone we wished. She explained, corrected, helped, and guided us. We developed relationships that still continue. We were no longer outsiders.

The Holy Spirit serves a similar yet much higher role for us. He transcends cultural and language limitations to bring us into a relationship with God. He, in a sense, "interprets" for us so that "we might know the things freely given to us by God" (1 Cor. 2:12). But He is more than a translator; He makes us a part of God's life. This bond is an internal experience that goes beyond dogma, investigation, and analysis.

Biblically, God's relationship with us is described as that of a loving Father to His children. Twice in the Scriptures the Holy Spirit is said to come into our hearts crying, "Abba! Father!" (Rom. 8:15; Gal. 4:6). The Spirit assures us of our privileged position in God's family: "The Spirit Himself bears witness with our spirit that we are children of God" (Rom. 8:16). How do we know that we are loved by God? "The love of God has been poured out within our hearts through the Holy Spirit who was given to us" (Rom. 5:5). True intimacy with God is accomplished only by the Holy Spirit.

The Holy Spirit provides access to God. In our prayer, the Spirit intercedes and heightens communications: "And in the same way the Spirit also helps our weakness; for we do not know how to pray as we should, but the Spirit Himself intercedes for us with groanings too deep for words" (Rom. 8:26).

The Outward Work of the Holy Spirit

A third role of the Holy Spirit's work is that He gives us a genuine unity with all other believers. All Christians are "baptized by the Spirit" into the body of Christ (1 Cor. 12:13). This special act is an objective work whereby each believer is placed into the same mystical relationship with Christ and each other. Whatever affects one member of the body affects the others as well: "And if one member suffers, all the members suffer with it; if one member is honored, all the members rejoice with it" (1 Cor. 12:26). When outsiders oppose Christians and persecute the church, it is the same as persecuting Christ Himself (Acts 9:4).

The outward ministry of the Holy Spirit includes His gifting members of the body of Christ for specific acts of ministry. These gifts involve everything from teaching and preaching to encouraging and financial giving (1 Cor. 12:8-10; Rom. 12:6-8; Eph. 4:11-13). Such abilities to serve are given to believers at the discretion of the Spirit. These gifts are for the good of the other members of the church, not for personal gain (1 Cor. 12:7, 11).

The outward work of the Holy Spirit binds all believers together in Christ. He enables us to relate to one another in a dynamic way. Our efforts are given a spiritual dimension which could not be attained at a human level.

The Gift of the Spirit

The presence of the Holy Spirit in each Christian's life is a gift from God. Those who have experienced His ministry in their lives find it easy to believe in the Holy Spirit. Yet, it is only through the Scriptures that we understand His existence, His presence, and His ministry. The Bible alone articulates for us His relationship to God the Father and the Son. This is a case where the authority of the Scriptures must be allowed to give us insight.

Most important, in His role as "another comforter," the Holy Spirit does for us what Jesus would do if He were here in person. Giving assurance, guidance for decision-making, conviction of sin, and encouragement to keep on in our faith, the Holy Spirit personally brings the presence of God into the life of every believer.

Discussion Questions

1. The Holy Spirit "seems extraneous to our understanding of God." Discuss this statement.

2. Why does the Bible contain so few explicit teachings about the Holy Spirit?

3. How can the Holy Spirit be a "person"?

4. The author compares the ministry of the Holy Spirit to that of a translator. In what ways is this true? (refer to 1 Cor. 2:10-16) In what ways is the Holy Spirit much more than a translator?

5. In many churches there is an emphasis on the work of the Holy Spirit in an individual's life (i.e., the gifts of the Spirit, etc.). How is this emphasis helpful? How can it potentially be detrimental?

Further Reading

Millard Erickson, *Christian Theology*, one volume ed. (Grand Rapids: Baker Book House, 1983–1985), pp. 865–886.

Michael Green, *I Believe in the Holy Spirit* (Grand Rapids: Wm. B. Eerdmans, 1975).

John Owen, *The Holy Spirit, His Gifts and Power* (Grand Rapids: Kregel Publications, 1954).

René Pache, *The Person and Work of the Holy Spirit* (Chicago: Moody Press, 1954).

CHAPTER EIGHT

Why Believe in the Trinity?

Off with your shoes, please, for the Holy Trinity is holy ground. Away with finely figured syllogisms and ordinary arithmetic: here, logic and mathematics do not suffice.

J. Kenneth Grider

Tell me how it is that in this room there are three candles but one light, and I will explain to you the mode of the divine existence.

John Wesley

Holy, holy, holy!
Lord God Almighty!
. . . God in three Persons,
Blessed Trinity.

So goes the hymn written by Reginald Heber. Christians have believed, taught, and sung that God is a Trinity since the Church began. This belief in a Triune God—Father, Son, and Holy Spirit—is distinctly Christian; no other religion holds anything close to such a belief.

The Trinity Rejected

"The Father, Son, and the Holy Spirit cannot be one God." As a good Mormon, Ken was expressing the teachings of the founder, Joseph Smith.

But Sheila was confused. "So you don't believe that they are equal—"

"Oh, no," Ken interrupted. "I didn't say that. They *are* equal, in a way."

Now Sheila was really perplexed. "Then you don't believe that they are God?"

"Yes, each one is God. The Father is God, Jesus is God, and the Holy Spirit is God. That's three gods."

"*Three* gods? I was always taught that there was only one. How many are there?"

Ken smiled. "Countless."

The Mormon view of polytheism ("many gods") is shared by Shinto and other religions that believe the universe is populated with gods. Thus, they reject the Christian concept of the Trinity, which maintains there is only one God.

On the other hand, some theistic religions reject the concept of the Trinity because, they say, it defies common sense. For example, the Jehovah's Witnesses claim that the doctrine of the Trinity is ridiculous and contrary to reason. They ask, "Whoever heard of three persons in one?" and beg for Christians to listen to reason.[1]

An Islamic writer also ridicules the "illogical" nature of belief in the Trinity. "If you ask a [Christian]-owned computer, 'God the Father, God the Son, and God the Holy Ghost—how many gods do they make?" it will immediately respond 'three' without blushing. It has no sympathy for its owner's desire to hear 'one.' "[2]

Others have not been so quick to discard the Trinity as meaningless. Instead, they have radically altered the traditional view of the Trinity in an attempt to make it easier to understand. The most popular explanation is that the Trinity is a description of the three ways, or modes, God has revealed Himself to man. This view of the Trinity, called *modalism,* is easy to illustrate. For example, I am a husband, a father, and a college professor, but I am still one person. I am performing in different roles, or modes, depending on when you see me.

The third-century theologian, Sabellius, claimed that God had made Himself known as the Father in creation and Law, the Son in incarnation and redemption, and the Holy Spirit in regeneration and sanctification. All three are ONE God, who unfolds His character in three successive ministries.

Contemporary liberal theology continues in this vein of modalism by emphasizing that God is not a Trinity in *essence* but a Trinity in *experience*. We encounter God through: the *love* of the Father, the *grace* of Jesus Christ, and the *fellowship* of the Holy Spirit.

Many have considered the traditional doctrine of the Trinity an embarrassment for Christianity, an absurd concoction of mythology, mystery religions, and Greek philosophy. Thomas Jefferson called the doctrine of the Trinity "incomprehensible jargon," and Matthew Arnold referred to it as a "fairytale."[3] Christians have often been accused of believing in three gods (tritheism) or of making God into a schizophrenic deity.

Because there is such a problem articulating the doctrine of the Trinity, wouldn't it be best to do away with it and try to describe God in more conventional terminology?

Why do Christians believe in the Trinity?

Difficulties with the Trinity

Why is the Trinity so hard for some to believe?

No doubt it is because the Trinity describes God in ways that defy "natural" reasoning. But this should not be surprising; such mental impasses have often occurred in many areas of study, particularly science.

For example, at the beginning of this century when scientists began to explore the makeup of the atom, they were astonished (and somewhat shaken) to discover a world that did not behave as they expected. The study of the subatomic world, known as quantum mechanics, reveals bizarre particles and forces that operate quite unlike the "billiard ball" universe that we can see.

The late Richard Feynman, Nobel laureate at Cal Tech, admitted, "I think it is safe to say that no one understands quantum mechanics."[4]

Since the tenets of quantum mechanics are beyond the understanding of the brightest minds, it is amazing that billions of dollars are spent in quantum research, which has produced technological wonders, such as computer chips and lasers. It is certainly clear that a complete understanding of a truth is not necessary for that truth to have practical and meaningful value. The same is true of the doctrine of the Trinity.

The traditional doctrine states clearly that God is three Persons yet one God. How can that be? A "person" is by definition one essence. To state that God is three Persons, then, is to assume that He is also three gods.

But is this correct reasoning? Must we be able to explain God so that He may be fully understood? No.

By saying that we believe in the Trinity, we acknowledge that God's nature may be described without being fully understood. We also acknowledge that because we are human, we face at least two limitations in our ability to comprehend God.

The first of these is *limited human thought.* We live at a level so far below the realm of God's essence that we are unable to comprehend the fullness of His character. C.S. Lewis beautifully illustrates this perspective:

> On the human level one person is one being, and any two persons are two separate beings—just as, in two dimensions (say on a flat sheet of paper) one square is one figure, and any two squares are two separate figures. On the Divine level you still find personalities; but up there you find them combined in new ways which we, who do not live on that level, cannot imagine.[5]

Because we live in a different dimension, much of what we can know about God is unintelligible to our normal ways of thinking. As a student of mathematics in the university, I spent a great deal of my time working with mathematical equations which describe shapes in an infinite dimensional space. Now I can easily conjure up pictures in my mind of one-, two-, and three-dimensional figures, but figures of four, five, six, a hundred, or a million dimensions? Our minds are incapable of such visualizations; yet, the calculations we carried out were meaningful in the realm of abstract mathematics, at least to mathematicians who understand that realm. Our understanding of the nature of God also cannot be visualized; so should we toss out the Trinity and accept something easier to understand? Of course not.

Our limited reasoning leads to our second limitation in comprehending the doctrine of the Trinity: *limited human language.* If we could mentally conceive of one God who is also three Persons, we might be able to express the concept. But since the idea is beyond even our imagination, how will we ever make it clear in human speech?

Many have attempted to use analogies to illustrate the Trinity, but most of these fall far short of explaining a threefold personality in one essence.

For example, the first analogy I learned in Sunday School was that the Trinity is like water, which can exist in a threefold manner: ice (solid), steam (gas), or water (liquid). This explanation actually fits into the modalistic view of the Trinity discussed earlier in this chapter. Furthermore, such an explanation ignores the concept of personality, which is crucial to our understanding of God.

Other analogies such as man (a trinity of body, soul, and spirit), the universe (space, matter, and time), and identical triplets (three persons from one embryo) all fail to communicate the essential feature of three persons in one essence.

Our main struggle may be with the idea of "persons." The word does not adequately convey all that is involved in the dynamics of the Trinity; yet, we have no better word to describe each member of the Trinity.

Admitting our limitations in understanding the Trinity does not mean that we are completely unable to understand the Godhead. Let's turn our attention to what we can understand about the Trinity.

The Trinity Described

The reason Christians hold so tenaciously to the doctrine of the Trinity is that the Scriptures offer no other alternative. Our understanding of the Trinity is truly an exercise in systematic theology. The word *Trinity* does not occur in the Bible, yet the overwhelming conclusion of biblical passages is that the Trinity is indeed three Persons but only one God.

Three parallel lines of truth, drawn from Scripture, lead us to affirm the reality of the Trinity:

1. God is ONE
2. Three separate Persons are called "God"
3. The three are ONE God

God Is One

At the heart of biblical faith is the belief that only one God exists. Israel's central confession was the acclamation "Hear, O Israel! The Lord is our God, the Lord is one!" (Deut. 6:4) The New Testament affirms this understanding of God: "We know that there is no such thing as an idol in the world, and that there is no God but one" (1 Cor. 8:4).

Paul included this doxology in his first letter to Timothy, "Now to the King eternal, immortal, invisible, the only God, be honor and glory forever and ever. Amen" (1 Tim. 1:17).

But within the understanding of the one God, the Bible displays a penchant for allowing God to be viewed as a plurality. Even in the Old Testament we see distinct hints of God being more than a static unity. For example, as we saw in chapter 7, plural pronouns are sometimes used to describe God: "Then God said, 'Let *Us* make man in *Our* image, according to *Our* likeness' " (Gen. 1:26, emphasis added; see also Gen. 3:22; 11:7). Isaiah was commissioned to his prophetic ministry when God asked, "Whom shall I send, and who will go for *Us*?" (Isa. 6:8, emphasis added)

Other references should be noted where the "Spirit of God" is given the attributes of deity (Gen. 6:3) and the

"Angel of the Lord," although a distinct personage from God, is worshiped and even called "Yahweh" (compare Gen. 16:11b with 16:13; see also Gen. 18:1–19:1).

It is noteworthy that certain passages appeal to God in a threefold manner.

> *The Lord* bless you, and keep you,
> *The Lord* make His face to shine on you,
> And be gracious to you;
> *The Lord* lift up His countenance on you,
> And give you peace (Num. 6:24-26).

Not to be forgotten is the triple doxology of the seraphim in Isaiah's vision: "Holy, holy, holy, is the Lord of hosts" (Isa. 6:3).

These references do not prove that the Trinity is presented in the Old Testament. To make this claim would be to speak far beyond the intended teachings. These passages do, however, lay the groundwork for the fuller revelation of the Trinity in the New Testament.

Three Separate Persons Are Called "God"

That the Father, Son, and Holy Spirit are individually called "God" has been discussed in previous chapters. It is sufficient at this point to mention that the biblical writers had no hesitation whatsoever in ascribing full deity to the Father (Matt. 11:25; Rom. 15:6), the Son (Rom. 9:5; Titus 2:13), and the Holy Spirit (2 Cor. 3:17).

It is also clear that each member of the Trinity is distinct and not simply another form, or mode, of God. This distinction will be made clearer in the next section.

The Three Are One God

The New Testament completes the portrait of God begun in the Old. At the outset of Jesus' ministry we see all three members of the Trinity present at His baptism:

> And after being baptized, Jesus went up immediately from the water; and behold, the heavens were opened, and He saw the Spirit of God descending as a dove, and coming upon Him, and behold, a voice out of the heavens, saying, "This is My beloved Son, in whom I am well-pleased" (Matt. 3:16-17).

Here, at *one time* and in *one place*, the three Persons of the Trinity were present and distinct. The Son is baptized, the Holy Spirit descends, and the Father speaks. This one brief picture of the Trinity together makes any form of modalism impossible.

Further, in the New Testament we see many instances where the persons of the Trinity perform similar yet distinct roles. Take, for example, Paul's description of the divine source of the spiritual gifts:

> Now there are varieties of gifts, but the same *Spirit.* And there are varieties of ministries, and the same *Lord.* And there are varieties of effects, but the same *God* who works all things in all persons (1 Cor. 12:4-6, emphasis added).

This same threefold pattern of joint ministry is found many times in the New Testament. (See 1 Cor. 6:11; Eph. 4:4-6; 2 Thes. 2:13-14; Acts 2:32-33; etc.) Even more interesting is the order in which the members of the Trinity are presented. We would think that the order would always be Father-Son-Spirit, but such is not the case. In fact, there seems to be no fixed order at all:

> God-Son-Spirit (Rom. 1:1-4);
> Christ-God-Spirit (2 Cor. 13:14);
> Christ-Spirit-God (1 Cor. 6:11);
> Spirit-Christ-God (1 Cor. 12:4-7)

This certainly implies an equality among the Godhead.[6]

Jesus Himself told his disciples to baptize new converts in the "name" (singular) of "the Father and the Son and the Holy Spirit" (Matt. 28:19). Note that Jesus does not say "names," which would imply that the Father, Son, and Holy Spirit were three gods.

The Indispensable Trinity

The importance of the doctrine of the Trinity must be considered from three perspectives: historical, theological, and practical.

The Historical Importance of the Trinity

Why must we consider the historical significance of the doctrine of the Trinity? The answer is that we want to discover what those closest to the time of Jesus believed. Did they believe in the Trinity? If so, why? How did they struggle with the doctrine, and in what ways has it been understood?

It is clear that the Trinity was immediately a part of the Christian confession. The earliest Christian creeds state a firm understanding of one God who consists of three Persons. The Apostle's Creed declares that Christians believe in the Father, the Son, and the Holy Spirit without seeing any need to fully explain their relationship. The theologian Tertullian (A.D. 200) described the Holy Spirit as "the sanctifier of the faith of those who believe in the Father and the Son and the Holy Spirit."[7]

The Nicene Creed (A.D. 325, revised A.D. 381) affirmed the full deity of each member of the Trinity. The most explicit pronouncement of the Trinity is found in the Athanasian Creed of the fourth century:

> . . . we worship one God in Trinity, and Trinity in unity; neither confounding the Persons nor dividing the substance, for there is one Person of the Father, another of the Son, and another of the Holy Ghost, but the Godhead of the Father, of the Son, and of the Holy

Ghost is one, the glory equal, the majesty co-eternal. . . .[8]

Without apology, the early fathers of the Christian church held to a belief in the Trinity. Why? Because they were driven by the evidence of Scripture to conclude that God is a triune Godhead. They wrestled with the Trinity for the same reasons we do today. But they allowed the Scriptures to dictate their doctrine, even when it went beyond their ability to fully understand. This has been the historic position of the Christian church throughout the centuries.

The Theological Importance of the Trinity

The members of the Godhead are equal in position and essence yet distinct in person and role. For example, the names "Father" and "Son" do not express a chronological relationship between the first two Persons of the Trinity. God, the Father, did not give birth to God, the Son. Rather, both terms are used to express a relationship between the two Persons that is eternal and personal.

Jesus is the "Son" in that He carries out a particular role. He is not inferior to the Father but merely performs different tasks.

In our society, one's job often determines one's significance and superiority. Though such distinctions are wrongly made, certain occupations carry a great amount of status in the eyes of many. For example, a bank president is superior to a janitor, even though the workers are equal in essence as human beings. We make the distinction between what one *does* and what one *is*.

But within the Trinity, such distinctions carry no implied superiority. Jesus is just as fully God as the Father and the Spirit. While He was on earth, Jesus was in essence God, but He limited Himself to become a human being in order to provide salvation for humanity.

Thus, the roles among the Trinity seem to describe a difference in function. The Father purposes (for example, redemption of mankind) and then expresses that purpose through the Son (His atonement) and then accomplishes that purpose through the Spirit (personal salvation).

The most important theological inference of the doctrine of the Trinity is directed toward the person of Jesus Christ. Those who reject the Trinity usually do so because they have first denied the deity of Christ. For this reason the Trinity often becomes a touchstone for orthodoxy. "What do you believe about the Trinity?" often boils down to "What do you believe about Jesus Christ?"

The Practical Importance of the Trinity

Can a doctrine as difficult as the Trinity have any practical value? Indeed it can. If nothing else, it shows us that God's nature goes beyond human understanding. Our "analysis" of God can only go so far before we find ourselves delving into mysteries we cannot fathom.

This serves as a reminder that we cannot make God simply a "superman" because His nature and His ways are beyond our understanding. Yet the beautiful truth is that God has spoken and revealed Himself to us. While we still struggle to understand what He has revealed, we can glory in what we do understand and long for the day when we shall know fully just as we have been fully known (1 Cor. 13:12).

But more personally, we can see that God is not a static unity but a dynamic fellowship. Within the Godhead there exists an interrelationship of love that has been expressed from eternity. Herein we can understand that "God is love" (1 John 4:8).

God did not learn to love; He has always loved. God did not create the world so He could personally relate with others; He has always related. God did not learn to communicate; He has always communicated.

We worship the Triune God who is the omnipotent Creator but who was also right here on earth as one of us and who now lives within us. This is the Trinity; this is our God.

Discussion Questions

1. Why is the Trinity so difficult to understand?

2. What are some ways the Trinity has been explained?

3. Is the Trinity a Christian concept only? Does the evidence of the Old Testament support the doctrine?

4. How does the New Testament explicitly reveal that God is three Persons yet one God?

5. Explain the statement: "One's understanding of the person of Jesus Christ affects one's view of the Trinity."

6. How may the roles of the Persons within the Trinity be distinguished?

Further Reading

Donald Bloesch, *The Battle for the Trinity: The Debate over Inclusive God-Language* (Ann Arbor, Mich.: Servant Publications, 1985).

Bruce Demarest and Gordon Lewis, *Integrative Theology*, vol. 1. (Grand Rapids: Zondervan Publishing House, 1987). See chapter 7: "God's Unity Includes Three Persons," pp. 249–289.

Millard Erickson, *Christian Theology*, one volume ed. (Grand Rapids: 1983–1985). Chapter 15: "God's Three-in-Oneness: The Trinity," pp. 321–344.

CHAPTER NINE

Why Believe in Salvation?

No deity will save us, we must save ourselves. Promises of immortal salvation or fear of eternal damnation are both illusory and harmful.
Humanist Manifesto II

No one can be redeemed by another. No God and no saint is able to shield a man from the consequences of his evil doings. Every one of us must become his own redeemer.
Subhadra Bhikshu

I am the door; if anyone enters through Me, he shall be saved.
John 10:9

"It's her fault!"
"It's his fault!"
"It's society's fault!"
"It's ________'s fault!"

Man has refused to take responsibility for his sin since Adam blamed Eve and Eve blamed the serpent. Everyone agrees that humanity has problems, but no one is willing to take responsibility for them. It has become fashionable to fault the government, big business, and even religion for the woes of our society. Not long ago I heard a television reporter interview the mother of a young man who had been arrested for committing a terrible crime. "He's a good boy," she said tearfully. "He just got in with the wrong friends."

In the West, we have adopted the Socratic maxim: "Knowledge is virtue." By this we imply that man's problems are due to ignorance, not evil. Man has not *fallen* from any previous state of innocence but is merely uninformed. Thus, education and knowledge are the keys to overcoming the ills of the world. "To know the good is to do the good."[1]

But we must ask, since knowledge is (supposedly) increasing at such a rapid rate, why are we not advancing equally in our morality, our enjoyment of life, and our well-being?

The injustice, suffering, pain, and sorrow that confront us every day serve as a constant reminder that something has gone wrong; and I know that I am part of the problem. In the evils of our society, I see mirrored my own pride, selfishness, and greed. This produces in me a sense of anxiety: What are the consequences? Must I pay for my sins?

I do not need more education; I need help.

This "help" that I seek is what the major religions of the world call "salvation." It is the belief that I must do something to free myself from the consequences of my moral deficiencies. People all over the world have different views as to what salvation is and how it may be obtained. Let's take a brief look at the major salvation schemes.

Different Views of Salvation

Hindus view salvation as the deliverance from the bondage of this world and from matter itself. Salvation provides release from the continuous cycle of birth and rebirth and a bodiless existence, free from the passions, desires, and needs of the flesh.

Salvation may be obtained through several means: acquiring knowledge (the removal of spiritual ignorance), renouncing the cares of this world, or living a life of devotion to spiritual aims (contemplation and meditation).[2]

Hindus look forward to a union with true reality, the divine Brahman.

Buddhism rejects Hinduism, except for the concepts of reincarnation and the goal of escaping the cycle of rebirth.

The core of Buddhist philosophy is found in the Four Noble Truths: suffering is a fact of existence; suffering is caused by selfish desires; release from suffering is possible; and the way of release is through the Eightfold Path.

The Eightfold Path is:

1. Right understanding
2. Right motivation
3. Right speech
4. Right conduct
5. Right vocation
6. Right effort
7. Right thinking
8. Right concentration

By adhering to the Eightfold Path, the Buddhist hopes to enter *Nirvana*, a state of "extinction" where all striving and personal suffering ceases.[3]

The *Islamic* view of salvation is a personal and very sensual existence in the world to come. The focus of salvation is to escape punishment in the future life. To achieve salvation, the Muslim must perform the five duties of Islam:

1. Recite the Islamic Creed ("There is no God but Allah, and Muhammed is his prophet");
2. Say the five stated daily prayers;
3. Fast;
4. Pay legal alms;
5. Take a pilgrimage to Mecca.

Even if Muslims faithfully fulfill these duties, they are still at the mercy of Allah, who ultimately grants salvation; so followers must carefully attend to every detail of the rituals.

Islamic salvation is entirely legalistic, aimed at achieving a release from the punishment of hell. In spite of the uncertainties, it is believed that all Muslims will be saved by virtue of their association with Islam.[4]

Common Beliefs

All of these religions hold several common beliefs regarding salvation.

1. *We have a need.* All views of salvation imply that man needs to be delivered. This need is present in the nature of man himself: selfish impulses which lead each person to focus on this-worldly needs and desires cause an insensitivity to true reality.

2. *Salvation is otherworldly.* The major religious views of salvation all point to a deliverance which is effected after death. For the Muslim, it is the release from the pains of eternal hell and an eternal existence with Allah. For the followers of Eastern religions, it is a release from the cycle of reincarnation and freedom from the bondage of the human body.

3. *Salvation is by our efforts.* The various religions differ in the specifics of how salvation is obtained. It may be through knowledge, and thus education is the path. It may be through a life of good works, a life of self-denial, or a life of meditation toward "enlightenment." Though the actual methods are different, it is agreed that by the sheer force of our wills we can overcome the limitations of our existence and obtain salvation from the world.

The Christian View of Salvation

Christianity does share some similarities with other world religions. Man *is* in need of deliverance. This life is *not* all there is. Beyond this realm a life exists that is eternal and free from the limitations and defilements of this world. Salvation in the Bible is described as eternal life with God, as opposed to the eternal punishment of hell.

But here Christianity parts company with these religions. Christianity adds another stipulation to the realization that man has a definite need for deliverance: Man is incapable of rescuing himself. By his own will and efforts, no matter how noble, man cannot save himself. Furthermore, this one life is all we get. There is no second chance, no reincarnation: "And inasmuch as it is appointed for men to die once and after this comes judgment" (Heb. 9:27). The future life is also an eternal *bodily* existence, not a bodiless, spiritual mode of being.

The Christian view of salvation may be understood by examining two major themes in Scripture: man's need and God's provision.

Man's Need

The nature of man. From the biblical perspective, man's problems are not the result of ignorance or any other deficiency. Rather, we have fallen away from God: "All of us like sheep have gone astray, each of us has turned to his own way" (Isa. 53:6). We are described as a "rebellious people, who walk in the way which is not good, following their own thoughts" (Isa. 65:2).

Initially, we were created *in* and *for* fellowship with God (Gen. 1:26-27). But mankind rebelled against its Creator (Gen. 3:1-7), and fellowship with God was broken. Every person shares in the reality of this rebellion against God.

Why every person since Adam has been a sinner is difficult to understand. It does not seem fair to suffer because of Adam's mistake. We were not there when he sinned; we didn't elect him to represent us. Yet, the Bible is very clear that we all sinned in Adam: "'Therefore, just as through one man sin entered into the world, and death through sin, and so death spread to all men, because all sinned" (Rom. 5:12).

But before any of us complain, we realize that we do sin now. I know that I am fully responsible for my sinful actions and am separated from God.

"I'm not a sinner," someone may say. "You won't see me killing or stealing or committing any of those horrible crimes." The problem with such a statement is that sin does not only consist of "horrible crimes." If we compare ourselves with the mass murderers of our society, we all look pretty good. But our comparative gaze is in the wrong direction. It's the black sheep that make the gray sheep look white.

If we compare ourselves with the moral perfection of God, we find that we fall short. Every small lie, evil thought, or selfish action reveals a flaw in our nature. "We all make mistakes," everyone admits. "Nobody's perfect." That's the point that God makes throughout the Bible.

Here is the crux of the salvation issue: we are alienated from God. The problem is that we have lost the intimate relationship with God for which we were created. The alienation is not merely an oversight on our part, but it is an estrangement of the worst kind. We have defied the One who made us. Our need, then, is not to adopt an acceptable lifestyle but to be reconciled to Him.

If two people have a conflict, the problem cannot be solved if both of them go about their lives and ignore whatever it was that caused the dispute. Even if they live in the same house and are physically close, the tension remains. There must be a change of heart, forgiveness, and acceptance before any reconciliation can take place.

In our relationship with God, *He* does not need a change of heart—*we* do. The enmity between us, caused by our sin, must be removed. We must be forgiven. We cannot merely educate ourselves or adopt a lifestyle of self-denial. We have to be changed within in order to be reconciled to Him.

Now if the problem was just with our *sins*, then we could conceivably just stop sinning and enter into fellowship with God. But anyone who has tried to stop sinning has found it impossible. Even if we could will ourselves to stop sinning, there is the problem of sins already committed in the past; how can we take care of them?

Our need goes beyond our sins. We sin because we are sinners. Every person stands condemned before God because we are sinful by nature (Eph. 2:1-3; Rom. 3:9-20). David cried out to God, "And do not enter into judgment with Thy servant, for in Thy sight no man living is righteous" (Ps. 143:2). This is a horrifying truth to many humanitarians. ("How can a sweet, innocent baby be evil?") But when we recognize that evil is that which is against the character and will of God, we see that all people, even from infancy, have a natural tendency to be independent and free from any restraints.

The Character of God. Because God is the type of Person that He is, He cannot just overlook man's sins and guilt. Why? Because He is the holy (Ex. 15:11; Lev. 11:44) and just God (Ps. 9:8; 96:13; 98:9). Suppose a local judge started to let lawbreakers off without having them pay any penalty. We might not appreciate his forgiving spirit if he let murderers and rapists go free. In fact, we would probably accuse the judge of not being "just." Justice involves paying a penalty when a crime has been committed.

God cannot let guilty humanity go free. He cannot judge unrighteously.

So what can man do to pay the penalty? The answer is "nothing." The end result of our sinfulness is death, "for the wages of sin is death" (Rom. 6:23). The death spoken of here refers to an eternal death; an eternal continuance of our alienation from God.

God's Provision

The chasm between God and man can be bridged only by God Himself. A major theme throughout the Bible is that salvation is uniquely of the Lord: "I, even I, am the Lord; and there is no saviour besides Me" (Isa. 43:11).

Activated by God. What motivates God to provide salvation? Just as God's character constrains Him to judge righteously, His character also compels Him to make provision to forgive and restore man. God is just, but He is also compassionate: "He has not dealt with us according to our sins, nor rewarded us according to our iniquities. For as high as the heavens are above the earth, so great is His loving-kindness toward those who fear Him" (Ps. 103:10-11).

God's loving concern for the welfare of His creation is summed up in the concepts of love, mercy, and grace. These terms often occur together when describing salvation: "But God, being rich in *mercy*, because of His great *love* with which He loved us, even when we were dead in our transgressions, made us alive together with Christ (by *grace* you have been saved)" (Eph. 2:4-5, emphasis added; see also Titus 3:4-7; Rom. 2:4).

"For God so loved the world" (John 3:16) is the first verse that many children learn. It portrays God as being intensely devoted to us. Rarely in the New Testament do we find the love of God for the world mentioned without some reference to the death of Jesus Christ: "But God demonstrates His own love toward us, in that while we were yet sinners, Christ died for us" (Rom. 5:8). (See 1 John 4:9-10.) God's love is a love in action.

Mercy refers to providing help for those who are in distress. Because of mankind's predicament, the whole race surely stands in a state of distress. But only God is in a position to rescue man.

Grace refers to providing help for those who are guilty. Here we find the love of God at its strongest. All of us, guilty and worthy of condemnation, are freely offered deliverance.

Accommodated by Jesus Christ. From the very outset of Jesus' ministry, it is made clear that He came to bring salvation to man (Matt. 1:21). His name, Jesus, means "God saves" and He described His mission as "seeking and saving the lost" (Luke 19:10).

The religions of the world say, "Follow these rules and you'll be OK."

But we need more than just another list of rules to follow; we need our debt paid and our hearts changed. Jesus not only told us the way of salvation, but He made that way possible through His death. His death was necessary in order to pay the penalty for the sin of mankind. This is the "good news" of the Gospel message: Christ has paid the penalty for our sin.

His payment for sin freed God to forgive the iniquity of mankind:

> This was to demonstrate His righteousness, because in the forbearance of God He passed over the sins previously committed; for the demonstration, I say, of His righteousness at the present time, *that He might be just and the justifier of the one who has faith in Jesus* (Rom. 3:25-26, emphasis added).

Now, Jesus is forever "the Savior of the world" (John 4:42). His death allows Him to bring together God and His estranged creation (1 Tim. 2:5). It is thus only through Jesus Christ that access to God is possible; He alone has taken away the enmity between God and man: "God was in Christ reconciling the world to Himself, not counting their trespasses against them" (2 Cor. 5:19).

Appropriated by Faith. God's provision of salvation as the payment for our sins must be appropriated by faith. The basis of our salvation is God's grace effected through the death of Jesus Christ. The benefits of Christ's atonement are accepted by faith as a free gift of God: "For by grace you have been saved through faith; and that not of yourselves, it is the gift of God (Eph. 2:8).

In chapter 2, I described faith as involving assent, trust, and commitment. When it comes to salvation, a person must first *believe* that Jesus died for the sins of the world. Our salvation is not based on human speculation or philosophy, but on a single, historical event.

Second, one must *trust* God that everything necessary for salvation has been accomplished. This is often difficult since we, by nature, want to add something to the work of God. But if we are going to come to God, we must come on

HIS terms, not ours.

Finally, we must *commit* ourselves to depend exclusively on the atonement of Jesus Christ for salvation. Good works add nothing to our standing before God (Eph. 2:9).

Paul laments the misguided attempts of the Israelites to establish their own righteousness. Even though they had a zeal for God, it was a zeal not founded on the knowledge of Jesus' atonement for sin (Rom. 10:1-4).

The salvation offered by God in the Scriptures is contrary to our way of thinking: *we* have sinned, so *we* must pay. But God's plan focuses on the character of God, so we should not be surprised if His way of salvation is not what we would expect. Thomas Aquinas wrote: "Human salvation demands the divine disclosure of truths surpassing reason."[5]

The Benefits of Salvation

Biblical salvation is a promise of eternal life with God. Peter speaks of our salvation which is "ready to be revealed in the last time" (1 Peter 1:5).

But salvation for the Christian involves more than just a life after death; there are benefits which accrue for believers the moment they place their faith in Christ. These benefits include not just a modification in attitude but also a genuine spiritual change in the life of the believer.

The first of these spiritual benefits is *justification*. Every believer is justified in the sight of God. This does not mean that each believer is actually righteous before God; rather that we are declared righteous since our penalty has been paid. In spite of the fact that we are guilty, God does not condemn us but justifies us on the basis of Christ's death (Rom. 3:25-26; 8:33-34).

From our perspective, justification doesn't seem "fair"; after all, we should have to pay for our wrongs. Yet, from God's side of the ledger, everything is taken care of because the debt has been paid by Another. Consider the example of an employee at a small store who had regularly taken money for himself from the cash register. Finally, his conscience broke him, and he confessed to the owner that he had taken what amounted to a significant sum over a period of years. Fully expecting to be prosecuted, the employee was stunned when a wealthy individual from the community repaid the store owner the entire sum.

Even though he was guilty and unable to repay such a large amount of money, the employee was freed from any penalty because of the provision of another. The store owner even allowed the employee to keep his job!

A second benefit of salvation is *regeneration*. The believer experiences a "spiritual rebirth" when he turns to the Lord for salvation. This is not merely "turning over a new leaf" but an actual reconstitution of one's nature: "Therefore if any man is in Christ, he is a new creature; the old things passed away; behold, new things have come (2 Cor. 5:17). Regeneration is effected by the Holy Spirit as He comes into a person's life when he believes. This is being "born of God" (John 1:13) or "born again" (1 Peter 1:3).

A third benefit of salvation is *adoption*, the act by which believers become the children of God. The estrangement from God is removed when we turn to Him through faith. In fact, salvation places us into the family of God. The presence of the Holy Spirit within us is the indication of our privileged position. He is called the "Spirit of adoption" who cries, "Abba! Father!" as He comes into our lives (Rom. 8:15; Gal. 4:6). Now we pray with confidence, "Our Father, who art in heaven."

Sanctification is a fourth benefit of salvation. The concept of sanctification involves being "set apart" for a particular purpose. At the moment of regeneration, each believer is set apart unto God and declared positionally righteous and holy in His sight. Again, this does not mean that the believer is *practically* righteous (that is, sinless), but that he has the position of holiness because Christ has paid the penalty for his sin. Therefore, all believers are called "saints," or "holy ones" (Rom. 1:7).

So Great a Salvation

Whereas the world focuses on what *we* can do to make ourselves acceptable, Christianity points to a gracious God who acts on our behalf.

The story is told of a young couple who endured severe financial difficulties after the husband lost his job. The financial strain began taking its toll on their relationship. Many times neighbors would hear them fighting late into the evening. The husband would often stalk out of the house, jump into the car, and drive away.

One afternoon, the couple was having a particularly noisy argument. The husband slammed the front door as he left. He started his car and screeched out of the driveway. Just as he reached the street he heard a sickening thud. His neighbor's little girl had ridden her tricycle across the driveway just as he pulled out. Long before the paramedics arrived it was clear that she was dead.

The people of the neighborhood were enraged. The couple stayed inside their home for a week, not knowing what to say or do.

The next week the father of the little girl appeared at the couple's door. Expecting the worst, the husband showed the father in.

With tears in his eyes, the father spoke calmly. "We understand that you and your wife are having financial problems. We had a $10,000 life insurance policy for our daughter. We want you to have the money." He handed a check to the young man.

Unbelievable? Yes. "Why, that young man ought to be in jail," many people would say. He was certainly deserving of some punishment. But not only was he forgiven, he was given great wealth.

This is the salvation provided for us by the grace of God. We stand guilty and deserving of punishment; yet God, because of His grace, not only forgives but also gives us eternal life as well. This is the great salvation of the Christian faith.

Discussion Questions

1. How can we tell that "there is something wrong with humanity?" In what ways does this point to a need for salvation?

2. What are the common characteristics of the salvation offered by the world religions?

3. Why are human effort and a salvation by works such common responses to man's sin?

4. How is the biblical view of salvation similar to that of the world religions? How is it different?

5. Biblically, salvation is described: "by grace through faith." What does this mean?

6. What is involved in accepting God's salvation "by faith"?

7. Salvation is present and future. Describe both aspects.

Further Reading

Millard Erickson, *Salvation: God's Amazing Plan* (Wheaton, Ill.: Victor Books, 1978).

Charles M. Horne, *Salvation* (Chicago: Moody Press, 1971).

CHAPTER TEN

Why Believe in Christ's Second Coming?

From the Scriptures we learn also of His second manifestation to us, glorious and divine indeed, when He shall come not in lowliness but in His proper glory, no longer in humiliation but in majesty.

Athanasius

Christ, having been offered once to bear the sins of many, will appear a second time, not to deal with sin but to save those who are eagerly waiting for Him.

Hebrews 9:28, RSV

Not long ago many people received a book: *88 Reasons Why the Rapture Could Be in 1988.*[1] The book was very clear about an earthshaking message—Christ will return on October 4, 1995. The author, former space engineer Edgar C. Whisenant, had worked out a detailed system to determine the exact date of Christ's Second Coming and then mailed his findings to people around the world so they could prepare themselves. When the Rapture failed to occur at the appointed time in the fall of 1988 (seven years before Christ's return), Whisenant began a revision of his calculations to predict a new date for the Second Advent.

He is not the first to make such predictions. J.B. Phillips recalls a man who warned the British Empire in 1934 that Christ would personally return on June 24. He was so convinced of his calculations that he stated if he were wrong, he would sink into well-merited obscurity. This latter prophecy turned out to be the correct one.[2]

We can all remember the doomsday predictions of the Jehovah's Witnesses, the Millerites, and a host of other prophetic groups. While unbelievers laugh at their predictive misfires, Christians are reminded that God has indeed promised a future intervention at the end of the world as we know it. We may not know *when*, but we do know it is certain.

The salvation provided by the coming of Jesus Christ has shaken the world's foundations but not changed its nature. Certainly, the Gospel has revolutionized the hearts of men and set societies and kingdoms on their ears, but evil, injustice, and suffering still permeate our lives.

On the human level, this life is most unsatisfying. Most of the world does not escape tragedy and intense suffering. I am an accident away from spending the rest of my natural life paralyzed or in pain. An undiagnosed disease may be present within me and snuff out my earthly existence within the year. Any number of calamities lurk on the fringes of my life as a constant reminder that this is a dying world.

As much as Christians like to speak of the sovereignty of God, we must admit there is a distinct tension within the world. We do not see all things in subjection to Him now (Heb. 2:8).

The Bible assures us that God will personally intervene and bring about the ultimate end of the world's suffering. He will establish His rule in which there will be no sorrow, suffering, disease, or death.

The first coming of Jesus Christ was the beginning of God's intervention. His miracles and message were a sign that "God has visited His people" (Luke 7:16). What Jesus accomplished in the way of relieving suffering and overcoming the limitations and sorrows in this life was but a brief preview of all that God intends to do. The future promises much more.

That Christ will return is not a minor theme of the Bible to be relegated to the appendix of our theological discussion. References to Christ's Second Advent occur eight times more often than those referring to His first coming. One third of all prophetic passages deal with His future return. The Second Coming of Christ is mentioned over 250 times in the New Testament and explained as the culmination of His work of total redemption.

To believe in His return is to accept at face value the overwhelming testimony of Christ and His disciples concerning the inevitable conclusion of redemption.

Universal Hope

The "blessed hope" of Christ's return is not limited to the pages of the biblical text. Many people outside of Christianity associate the end of the world with some concept of Christ's return.

Even popular religions pick up on this theme. Many proponents of New Age thinking have tried to assimilate the hope of Christ's return with the beliefs of other religions. In fact, many New Agers believe that the "Christ" is already in the process of returning. On April 25, 1982, a full-page advertisement in more than twenty major newspapers around the world boldly proclaimed: **"THE CHRIST IS NOW HERE."** The half-million-dollar ad went on to describe the presence of a currently undiscovered "Lord Maitreya." Somewhere in the world he has been teaching a gospel of justice, peace, and unity since 1977. Through his spiritual insight and power, this savior will bring about a new world order. He is the Christ of the Christians, the Messiah of the Jews, the Fifth Buddha of the Buddhists, the Imam Mahdi of the Muslims, and the Krishna of the Hindus.[3]

But the Second Coming of Jesus Christ cannot be syncretized to fit all religious schemes. The uniqueness of Christ as God incarnate ensures that His return will be just as unique.

The restoration He promises means that the drudgery and despair of this life will be overcome by the actual presence of God with us.

Differing Views of His Return

How will Jesus return? When will He return?

Many refuse to regard Christ's return as a future, world-embracing event. They claim that biblical references to His Second Advent describe events that have already occurred or are currently taking place.

Some believe that the promises of the Second Coming were fulfilled at Pentecost (Acts 2:1-13). They believe that when the Holy Spirit came at Pentecost, the Second Coming of Christ was initiated. Now the Holy Spirit, "another Comforter" (John 14:16), dwells within us, fulfilling the ministry of Christ upon the earth in the present time.

Others believe that Christ's return is fulfilled on a more personal basis. They interpret the Second Coming as a continuing ministry of Christ coming into the lives of believers when they trust in Him. The purpose of His First Advent was to walk among men and atone for sin; the purpose of His Second Advent was to dwell within men by entering their hearts at salvation.

Still others believe that when Christians die, the Lord, in a sense, "returns" to usher them into the presence of God and fulfill the promise of eternal life. As Stephen saw the enthroned Christ standing to welcome him into heaven (Acts 7:55-56), it is believed that every Christian experiences the Second Coming of Christ at death.

While these views have some truth to them, they do not fully explain the vast number of biblical references describing the Second Coming of Christ.

How *does* the Bible picture the Second Advent of Christ?

CHRIST'S RETURN: THE BIBLICAL DRAMA

The Second Coming of Christ is an event that is portrayed as more than just His "coming [again]" (Matt. 24:3; 1 Cor. 15:23; 2 Thes. 2:1). The Lord's return is also described as His "appearing" (Titus 2:13) and His "revelation" (2 Thes. 1:7; 1 Peter 1:7), terms that emphasize the visible and physical nature of His advent.

Jesus is now in heaven "until the period of restoration of all things about which God spoke by the mouth of His holy prophets from ancient time" (Acts 3:21). His return will be the marked beginning of this period of restoration.

The Nature of His Return

The time of the Lord's return is one of the great mysteries of the Bible. Even Jesus Himself, in the limitations imposed by His incarnation, did not know the hour of His return (Matt. 24:36). The "Day of the Lord," the inception of God's ultimate intervention into human affairs, will come swiftly and unexpectedly as a "thief in the night" (1 Thes. 5:2).

For the last thirty years or so, discerning the "signs of His coming" has been a popular (and profitable!) pastime for many. While quite a few elaborate schemes of end-time events border on the absurd, we cannot dismiss the evidence Jesus gives concerning His appearance.

He states: "Now learn the parable from the fig tree: when its branch has already become tender, and puts forth its leaves, you know that summer is near; even so you too, when you see all these things, recognize that He is near, right at the door" (Matt. 24:32-33).

Jesus even rebukes the Jewish leaders for their ability to discern the signs of weather changes better than the signs of God's dealing with the world (Matt. 16:1-4).

Some of the events described as preceding the Lord's return are general in nature and could depict a number of historical periods. Among these signs are occultic activity (1 Tim. 4:1), earthquakes and other natural disasters (Luke 21:10-11), persecution of believers (Matt. 24:9-10), an increase in crime (Matt. 24:12; Luke 21:9), the appearance of false Messiahs (1 John 4:3; Matt. 24:10-11), and an overall increase of tribulation in the world (Matt. 24:21, 24).

In fact, Christ's return is said to occur at a time "just like the days of Noah" (Matt. 24:37). Jesus portrays this period as a time when people were "eating and drinking . . . marrying and giving in marriage" (Matt. 24:38). They had no hint of the coming calamity until it was upon them. Jesus warned His disciples, "For this reason you be ready too; for the Son of man is coming at an hour when you do not think He will" (Matt. 24:44).

When the Lord does return, the event will be anything but secret. The Lord is said to return in the clouds with the heavenly host, accompanied by natural catastrophes and celestial calamities (Mark 8:38; 13:26). Everything in the world will stop. All eyes will turn to the sky as the Lord Himself comes back to the earth as He promised.

The Reason for His Return

Why does Jesus need to return?

He will return because redemption is not complete. The final end of redemption is not merely the reconciliation of mankind to God but also a complete restoration of all creation.

The Scriptures make it clear that Christ's reign has already begun (Col. 1:13; Acts 28:23, 31). But, as we noted before, "we do not yet see all things subjected to Him" (Heb. 2:8). There is an "already/not yet" tension that permeates the Bible. Our present salvation is but a down payment of the full redemption promised by God. Even creation itself "groans" for its restoration from the futility of decay, rust, and death (Rom. 8:19-22).

A second reason for the Lord's return is to judge humanity in order to finalize each individual's destiny. While the Bible describes numerous judgments to be carried out in the end times, the ultimate judgment will concern eternal life and rewards for those who are His children, and eternal death and punishment for those who have rejected Him (see chapter 11).

> But when the Son of man comes in His glory, and all the angels with Him, then He will sit on His glorious throne. And all the nations will be gathered before Him; and He will separate them from one another, as

the shepherd separates the sheep from the goats (Matt. 25:31-32).

Associated with this judgment is a third major purpose for Christ's return: the resurrection of all humanity. The promise of eternal existence includes a *bodily* existence for both the good and the evil. Jesus predicted: "An hour is coming, in which all who are in the tombs shall hear His voice and shall come forth; those who did the good deeds to a resurrection of life, those who committed the evil deeds to a resurrection of judgment" (John 5:28-29).

Jesus and the Kingdom

We cannot consider the Second Coming of Christ apart from His reign as King. His return is portrayed as a regal procession and enthronement of a monarch over His conquered realm.

The reign of Jesus has been variously understood by interpreters. Assumed to last 1,000 years (Rev. 20:1-7), His earthly rule is generally called the Millennium, a term based on the Latin root *mille* for 1,000. However, not everyone agrees when and how Christ will carry out this reign. Let's look at four of the major views concerning Christ's earthly reign.

Realized Millennialism

Those who hold to a realized millennialism view believe that there is no literal return of Christ to earth. They tell us that we should not look to the future for God's kingdom—the future is now! The era of God's rule began when Jesus appeared in human history, bringing with Him the message of divine love and power. Now Christ rules in the hearts of men and women who spread the ever-growing kingdom message of the Gospel.[4]

Amillennialism

As the name implies, amillennialists believe that there will not be a literal 1,000-year reign of Christ on earth ("a" [no] + millennium). The Old Testament promise of the kingdom of the Jews and the 1,000-year period mentioned in Revelation 20 are viewed simply as metaphorical descriptions of a nonpolitical reign of Christ. He now rules sovereignly through the church or reigns in heaven. Christ's Second Coming will end this period of time and usher in the eternal state.[5]

Postmillennialism

Postmillennialists are the eschatological optimists. They believe that the influence of the church and the Gospel message will spread over the earth and eventually bring in a time of peace and prosperity. This age will be the kingdom of God promised in the Scriptures. At the conclusion of this kingdom era Jesus Christ will return. Thus, Christ's Second Coming is after ("post") the Millennium. After His glorious return, Christ will institute the new heaven and new earth.[6]

Premillennialism

Premillennialists believe that Christ will return ("pre" [before] + millennium) and set up a literal rule on the earth lasting 1,000 years. Those who hold this view understand the Old Testament promises to Israel as being literally fulfilled in the future. The Second Coming of Christ described in Revelation 19 is followed by the 1,000-year reign depicted in Revelation 20.[7]

Sorting through these various views is not easy. Often, the major differences are over the prophetic biblical passages. For example, if one takes the promises to Israel to be fulfilled as they seem to be described in the Old Testament (i.e., a literal Jewish nation dwelling in Palestine [Isa. 9:1-7; 11:1-9; Micah 4:1-7]), then a premillennial position is warranted. Many feel this fits in best with the common Jewish expectation of the Messiah who will come and set up the promised eternal kingdom of David (2 Sam. 7:12-16).

If, however, the promises made to Israel are seen to portray a nonliteral, spiritual kingdom, then an amillennial position is the result. The New Testament church is thus seen as receiving the benefits of the prophetic covenants initially given to Israel in the Old Testament.

Furthermore, if one interprets the predictions of universal tribulation to describe only first-century events, then a postmillennial position is possible.

The problem is not having too little biblical information but having too much! Almost every New Testament book has some mention of the Lord's return, and some books (such as the Thessalonian epistles) are devoted to eschatological themes. Add to this the bulk of the Old Testament prophecies relating to the future messianic kingdom, and there is no lack of scriptural data.

We must remember that the major focus of doctrinal purity in the Bible is on the person and work of Jesus Christ (1 John 4:1-3) and the way of salvation by grace (Gal. 1:6-9). The details of eschatology were never seen as a test for orthodoxy.

Is it important, then, to search the Scriptures to understand future events? Yes.

Without the promises of the future, the Christian message is incomplete. God is moving history somewhere—and only the Scriptures tell us where. In our world, in which half of all children under twelve fear that a nuclear war will rob them of their teenage years, the message of God's future plans gives hope.

The Beginning of the End

The most important truth is this: Jesus is coming back. When Jesus was taken up into the clouds at His ascension, the angels told the disciples, "Men of Galilee, why do you stand looking up into the sky? This Jesus, who has been taken up from you into heaven, will come in just the same way as you have watched Him go into heaven" (Acts 1:11). As the first-century Christians began anticipating the Lord's return, a common expression of greeting was "Maranatha!" ("O Lord, come back!"; see 1 Cor. 16:22)

The truth of His return and our gathering to Him stands as the climactic conclusion to all that God has promised. It is the beginning of the end; the final restoration of all creation.

How does this future event affect us today? It gives meaning to our lives and efforts: "Your toil is not in vain in the Lord" (1 Cor. 15:58). There is an eternal significance to who we are and what we do. It also serves as a motivation to stand firm in our faithfulness and holiness, knowing that one day we shall see Christ who died for us (1 John 3:3).

When Christ returns, our faith shall become sight. The drudgery and suffering of this life will disappear with one powerful sweep of heavenly procession.

"Beloved, now we are children of God, and it has not appeared as yet what we shall be. We know that when He appears, we shall be like Him, because we shall see Him just as He is" (1 John 3:2).

Maranatha!

Discussion Questions

1. Why is the Second Coming of Christ called "the blessed hope"?

2. What is the significance of Christ's return as far as our salvation is concerned?

3. What are the "signs of His coming"?

4. *Why* is Jesus returning to the earth?

5. What are the major views concerning the time and manner of Christ's return? Why is there such disagreement among Christians about the details of end-time events?

Further Reading

Millard J. Erickson, *Contemporary Options in Eschatology* (Grand Rapids: Baker Book House, 1977).

Gleason Archer, Paul Feinberg, Douglas Moo, Richard Reiter, *The Rapture: Pre-, Mid-, or Post-Tribulational?* (Grand Rapids: Zondervan Publishing House, 1984).

Robert G. Clouse, ed., *The Meaning of the Millennium: Four Views* (Downers Grove, Ill.: InterVarsity Press, 1977).

CHAPTER ELEVEN

Why Believe in Heaven and Hell?

The belief in the immortality of the human soul is a dogma which is in hopeless contradiction with the most solid empirical truths of modern science.

Ernst H. Haeckel

Everything science has taught me—and continues to teach me—strengthens my belief in the continuity of our spiritual existence after death.

Wernher von Braun

June took a deep breath. *One more to go*, she thought to herself. Opening the hospital-room door, she smiled broadly. "Good evening, Mr. Vickers! How are you?"

The sound of the respirator echoed in the room. Harry Vickers rolled his eyes toward June, his face expressionless. After checking his chart, making small talk as she did, June noticed a crumpled piece of paper in Mr. Vicker's hand.

"Is this for me?" she asked.

Harry Vickers nodded.

Taking the paper, she read the almost illegible scrawl: *How much longer?*

June's heart raced. She looked into Mr. Vicker's eyes and saw fear mixed with pain.

"It's OK, Mr. Vickers. You're just tired. You need your rest. I'll see you tomorrow afternoon."

In the hallway, June slumped into a chair. "O God," she prayed, "please don't let him die on my shift."

One of the most difficult problems medical professionals face today is caring for the terminally ill. The medical procedures are not the difficulty. The struggle is helping patients cope with fear of the unknown in their last days.

Our world is not the land of the living but the land of the dying. Death is the inevitable end of every living thing, and the mystery that lies beyond our last heartbeat is the source of our greatest fears.

In spite of a natural anxiety about death itself, many people have a real sense of hope that goes beyond the grave. Belief in immortality is at the core of every human religious aspiration.

Christianity teaches that every person has an ultimate and eternal destination in either one of two places: heaven or hell. A recent Gallup poll showed that 84 percent of Americans believe in heaven (and 66 percent believe they are going there) while fewer than half believe in the existence of hell.[1] Is it possible to have one without the other? Let's look at the negative side first.

What about Hell?

The doctrine of hell is difficult to square with our understanding of a loving and good God. How could a Being with any sense of fairness commit people of His own creation to suffer torment for eternity? Atheist philosopher Anthony Flew asks this question many times when he debates Christians and has not received what he considers an adequate answer.

We must admit that Christianity is one of the few religions that holds to a doctrine of hell. Hell is not the sort of place that man would naturally create in his religions—it is too awful.

There has been a movement by many to dismiss the doctrine of hell as ungodly and unbiblical. Some prefer to believe that the punishment for rejecting God and His offer of eternal life is not everlasting torment but complete eradication. Thus, when John states "Whoever believes in Him [Christ] will not perish, but have eternal life" (John 3:16), the two options are eternal life with God or perishing—that is, *annihilation.* For example, Edward Fudge writes, "The 'everlasting destruction' [2 Thes. 1:9] of the wicked does not mean that Christ will be forever in the process of destroying them but that their destruction, once accomplished, will be forever. . . . Never, ever after, in all eternity, will the wicked be."[2]

Similar to the concept of annihilation is the concept of *conditional immortality.* Those who hold this view believe that all human beings cease to exist at death unless they are given eternal life by God. The phrase "The wages of sin is death" (Rom. 6:23) refers not to spiritual death but to total extinction of the person. The proponents of this position teach that when a person comes to Christ, he or she receives eternal life as a gift. Thus, immortality is conditioned upon one's acceptance of Christ: believers live forever with God; unbelievers die and are extinguished.

These views do not match up with the biblical evidence. Jesus warned His disciples that the ultimate fear of this life is not death "but the One who . . . has authority to cast into hell" (Luke 12:5). If death for the unbeliever means extinction, then Jesus' warning makes no sense.

What Does the Bible Say about Hell?

Hell is poetically described in the Bible as the place "where the worm does not die and the fire is not quenched" (Mark 9:48) and a place of "weeping and gnashing of teeth" (Matt. 13:50).

The Greek word used for "hell" in the Old Testament is *gehenna,* the name of the Valley of Benhinnom west of Jerusalem where Ahaz and Manasseh sacrificed children to the god Moloch (2 Chron. 28:3; 33:6). King Josiah abolished these sacrifices, and since then the valley has been used as a garbage dump for the city of Jerusalem. The condition of the valley presents a poignant picture: worms, maggots, smoldering fires, and smoke. In later Jewish thought the valley was used to convey the idea of a place of everlasting torment for the wicked (1 Enoch 27:2; 4 Ezra 7:36).

In the Parable of Lazarus and the Rich Man, Jesus describes the state of both men after death. The righteous Lazarus is seen reclining at a banquet with Abraham while the rich man finds himself in torment (Luke 16:19-31). The purpose of this parable is not to teach the ultimate end of people after death; yet the picture Jesus draws for us no doubt is an accurate portrayal.

Questions about hell are disturbing, but we cannot ignore the powerful presentation of hell as the inevitable end for those who reject the Lord. Three truths must be kept in mind:

1. God continues to reveal His character and His will through all He has made. Creation and conscience are not passive indicators of God's presence in the universe but formidable instruments in the hands of the Holy Spirit to convince each person of his need for God.
2. God seeks to lead people to Himself through His kindness and patience (Rom. 2:4). While being reconciled to God in order to avoid the judgment of hell can be an honest motivation, the biblical emphasis is upon mankind being reconciled to God for the enjoyment of the eternal fellowship for which we were created.
3. God must be fair, righteous, and just. He cannot deny His own character. If He could, then the death of Jesus Christ would have been unnecessary. Whatever the ultimate end of all things, no person will be able to say, "God, You were not fair!"

Hell is a place that is as indescribable as heaven. It is an unrelenting isolation, torment, and darkness. The constant and conscious realization of the finality of the judgment will only heighten the anguish. Hell is, in the words of Thomas Hobbes, "Truth seen too late."

Heaven Can't Wait

On the other side of eternity is the existence of heaven. Heaven is usually described as the place of eternal life and happiness. But not everyone thinks that heaven is such a good idea.

In spite of its universal appeal, many feel that the belief in heaven is a "pie-in-the-sky-when-you-die" philosophy that fails to match up to reality. How can we have any assurance of things we cannot see? Are we not fooling ourselves into thinking that we will live forever? Let's look at three major objections to the belief in heaven.

1. "There Is No Proof that Heaven Exists."

Imagine an isolated South American tribe that knows nothing of the outside world. No one in the tribe has ever seen or heard of modern societies, cities, or jet planes. Then a Peace Corps volunteer appears and describes the wonders of worlds far away. He tells them of people who do not grow or catch their own food, yet have more than enough to eat; of buildings that reach up into the sky; and of gleaming, silver birds that carry people from place to place through the air.

At first, the people do not believe that such a world exists, but in time the superior knowledge and abilities of the outsider begin to convince them that his words are true. His message influences the way the people view their world. Many of these new concepts and images find their way into the vocabulary and thinking of the tribe.

Christians believe that our world was visited by an Outsider who told us of the wonders of the world beyond. Jesus let us in on the secrets of heaven and gave us a glimpse of what is out there for us.

He did more than merely teach us about heaven; His own death and resurrection forever stand as validations that death is NOT the end of all things for all people.

Add to this the internal feeling that we have that this life is not all there is. Indeed we have "eternity in our hearts" (Ecc. 3:11). This has been expressed by many thinkers and writers throughout history. The Jewish writer of the Wisdom of Solomon proclaimed, "God created man to be immortal, and made him to be an image of His own eternity" (Wisdom 2:23).

Socrates saw many analogies in everyday life that gave him the confidence that life continues after death: butterflies bursting forth from cocoons, and leaves growing on "winter-dead" trees. Immanuel Kant, the great German philosopher, was convinced of the reality of heaven because justice cannot be carried out in this life alone: every wrong must be made right; every good must be rewarded. There must be a life after this in order to set all things right.

2. "Belief in Heaven Takes Our Eyes off This World."

Merrill Holste, who calls himself the "angry atheist," is particularly angry at Christians because of their belief in heaven. "We atheists are realists," he says. "We bet everything on the present life with its certain, though modest, rewards. The Christian, on the other hand, gambles on an improbable hereafter . . . in the hope of gaining more—just like the silly pooch in Aesop's fable who lost a bone trying to get a bigger one."[3]

Like the angry atheist, those who reject the idea of heaven feel that it takes away a person's concentration on this life—the here and now. For this reason, heaven cannot be a reality since it robs us of a proper focus on our present existence. Promises of a future eternal life of joy are an illusion used to foster false hope.

Karl Marx taught that government and religion were employed by the wealthy few to keep the poorer and less educated majority in check. The poor could be subdued and satisfied with very little in this life by promising them the wealth of heaven. This promise encouraged the poor to endure their miserable existence in this present world.

This line of thinking is similar to the philosophy of Epicurus (341–270 B.C.). He taught that religion produces only fear by claiming that the gods have some influence over a person's life (and afterlife). This fear keeps the individual from fully enjoying life and causes him to refrain from certain pleasures because of possible future judgment.

But the Christian perspective of heaven is much different than that described by Epicurus or Marx. The reality of heaven allows the believer to view life as it really is: eternal. This life is not all there is. Thoughts of heaven usually produce a desire to live life to the fullest here and now This of course does not mean that we indulge in gross pleasures, for this results in nothing more than spiritual, psychological, and social anarchy. Rather, the Christian is able to live a life that is enjoyable because of the liberation of knowing the truth. The anonymous maxim is true: "He who thinks most of heaven will do most for earth."

3. "Heaven Is Only a Psychological Projection of Wishful Thinking."

Sigmund Freud thought that religious aspirations were merely projections of our intense desire for a perfect father and our aversion to death.

Freud's claim leads to the conclusion that if this life is all there is, then my existence has no ultimate meaning. Furthermore, if there is no God or life after death, then I will not be held accountable for my actions. I have no reason to live a moral life or care for the needs of those around me. I know that the highest pleasures of life are found in fulfilling myself.

In the Bible, one who adopts such a pleasure-oriented, self-seeking philosophy of life is called a fool: "And I will say to my soul, 'Soul, you have many goods laid up for many years to come; take your ease, eat, drink, and be merry.' But God said unto him, 'You fool! This very night your soul is required of you; and now who will own what you have prepared?'" (Luke 12:19-20) Our lives are not meaningless blips on a screen that no one is watching; every person will give account of himself before the One who gave him life.

There is nothing wrong with eating, drinking, and making merry, but if this is the sole substance of life, there is nothing but emptiness and despair. We are no better than the animals who seek only to fill their bellies and litters.

The Christian View of Heaven

For the Christian, death is not a period but a comma. Death is the door to a newer and better existence, the promise of eternal life with the Father in heaven.

It is interesting that the Bible has very little to say about what heaven is actually like. Jesus tells His disciples that the wonders of the heavenly existence go beyond human knowledge and comprehension (1 Cor. 2:9). Peter writes:

> Blessed be the God and Father of our Lord Jesus Christ, who according to His great mercy has caused us to be born again to a living hope through the resurrection of Jesus Christ from the dead, to obtain *an inheritance which is imperishable and undefiled and will not fade away, reserved in heaven for you,* who are protected by the power of God through faith for a salvation ready to be revealed in the last time" (1 Peter 1:3-5, emphasis added).

No doubt heaven is a place where the impediments and limitations of this life will not exist. No more decaying, rotting, or rusting. Life, then, is truly eternal both in its length and in its quality.

In this sense, the "kingdom of heaven" was presented through the ministry of Jesus Christ. While he lived on earth, he was continually correcting the decadent nature of human existence by giving health where there was disease, life where there was death, and peace where there was turmoil.

The Rest of the Story: Bodily Resurrection

The Eastern religions promise us a future that is impersonal and devoid of individuality, an extinction of "me" as I become part of the cosmic "It."

Christianity promises us an eternal, *bodily* existence.

The thought of living eternally as "spirits" is not present ın the biblical writings.

In heaven we will be given new bodies like the resurrected body of Jesus. Paul tells the Philippians: "For our citizenship is in heaven, from which also we eagerly wait for a Saviour, the Lord Jesus Christ; who will transform the body of our humble state into conformity with the body of His glory, by the exertion of the power that He has even to subject all things to Himself" (Phil. 3:20-21).

The reality of the future resurrection promises a life where every human frailty is removed. It is a world where Fanny Crosby sees, Helen Keller sings, and Joni Eareckson Tada runs.

Former French President Charles de Gaulle had a daughter who was born severely retarded. Little Anne required constant care from General de Gaulle and his wife, who lovingly devoted their time to her. Although de Gaulle wore a rough exterior in public, many were impressed with the sensitivity and tenderness he expressed to his daughter. He often held her hand at night until she fell asleep.

When Anne turned twenty, she contracted a lung ailment and died. After her funeral and burial, de Gaulle turned to his wife and said, "Now at last, our child is just like all children."[4]

In heaven there will be a marked continuation of who we are in this life. But our new bodies will be "incorruptible, immortal, and imperishable" (1 Cor. 15:50-54). Death will no longer be the menacing villain waiting to assault us. "Death is swallowed up in victory" (1 Cor. 15:54).

When will this happen? Some believe that we receive our new bodies immediately after death; however, the Bible seems to point to a climactic moment in the future when all those who have died in the faith will receive their imperishable bodies: "Behold, I tell you a mystery; we shall not all sleep, but we shall all be changed, in a moment, in the twinkling of an eye, at the last trumpet; for the trumpet will sound, and the dead will be raised imperishable, and we shall be changed" (1 Cor. 15:51-53). Here Paul makes a distinction between those who have died and those who are alive "at the last trumpet." The dead shall be raised imperishable while those who are alive will be "changed."

Other passages make it clear our resurrection is to be associated with the return of the Lord (1 Thes. 4:13-18; 1 John 3:2; John 5:28-29). The restoration of God's visible rule on the earth will include the resurrection of all the saints to live and reign with Him forever.

The Future Hope

Why believe in heaven?

Believing in heaven assures us that there will be ultimate justice in the world, that everything will be made right.

Heaven is such a major theme of the New Testament that to take out references to it would alter almost every page of the text.

Most important, heaven is where God is and where we want to be, not as ethereal spirits but as real human beings in a genuine and vital relationship with God and His people.

The truth of the future hope for the believer is so much a part of the Christian faith that if it is not true, the whole Gospel message must be discarded. Paul goes so far as to claim that if there is no resurrection, our faith is both empty and fruitless (1 Cor. 15:12-19). If our faith only affects this life on earth, then we are, as Paul states, "of all men most to be pitied" (1 Cor. 15:19).

The one shining star that pierces through the cloud of uncertainty regarding heaven is the historical reality of the resurrection of Jesus Christ. If *He* has been raised from the dead, then we shall be raised too. He is the "first fruits" of those who have died in faith (1 Cor. 15:20). His resurrection guarantees that all of us who are "in Him" shall be raised "with Him" in the likeness of His resurrection.

Eternal, joyful fellowship with God is the climactic ending of God's love story. Those who are His shall live with

Him forever. "He shall wipe away every tear from their eyes; and there shall no longer be any death; there shall no longer be any mourning, or crying, or pain; the first things have passed away" (Rev. 21:4).

Discussion Questions

1. Why do many people want to do away with the doctrine of hell?

2. Why do you think so many people believe in life after death?

3. What are the major objections to a belief in heaven? How do you answer these objections?

4. Why does the Bible usually describe what heaven is NOT rather than what it IS?

5. How does the reality of our future resurrection give us some insight into the nature of heaven?

6. What do you think we will look like in heaven? Will we recognize our family and friends?

Further Reading

Murray J. Harris, *Raised Immortal: Resurrection and Immortality in the New Testament* (Grand Rapids: Eerdmans, 1985).

Peter Toon, *Heaven and Hell: A Biblical and Theological Overview* (Nashville: Thomas Nelson, 1986).

Wilbur M. Smith, *The Biblical Doctrine of Heaven* (Chicago: Moody Press, 1968).

CHAPTER TWELVE

What about Those Who Disagree?

No matter what side of an argument you're on, you always find some people on your side that you wish were on the other side.
Jascha Heifetz

Discussion is an exchange of knowledge; argument an exchange of ignorance.
Robert Quillen

If you can't answer a man's argument, all is not lost; you can still call him vile names.
Elbert Hubbard

A delightful story is told about George Whitefield and John Wesley, two of the greatest preachers who ever lived. Both were intellectually brilliant, and both were responsible for thousands coming to Christ during the great revivals of the eighteenth century.

But theologically Whitefield and Wesley had serious disagreements. Whitefield was an unflinching Calvinist; Wesley was strongly Arminian. Their differences made for great discussion among the common people who often chose sides according to which preacher they thought was teaching "the truth."

Whitefield was once questioned: "Mr. Whitefield, do you believe that you will see John Wesley in heaven?"

George Whitefield thought for a moment and replied with an emphatic "No!" Then he went on, "John Wesley shall be so close to the throne of God that I shan't catch a glimpse of him."

Wesley and Whitefield held strongly to their positions, but they were tough-minded enough to know that members of God's family often disagree.

Once we commit ourselves to a truth, we are in a position to be opposed by anyone who disagrees. Such disputes arise both from within the Christian family as well as from without. In either case, Christians must respond in a biblical manner.

How we respond is usually determined by the approach we take to our faith. For the Christian, there are at least three possibilities: the *narrow-minded* approach, the *free-minded* approach, and the *tough-minded* approach.

Narrow-minded, Free-minded, Tough-minded?

If I take a *narrow-minded* approach to my faith, I will not allow myself to hear or read anything that disagrees with my views. I am concerned that if I expose myself to other positions, my thinking may become defective. I judge other people by my standard of "correct belief" (which means, "believing like me").

For example, a pastor once told me that I would never speak in his church "because you are not one of us." The fact that we had different views on a minor point of theology placed me outside his circle of faith.

Narrow-minded Christians are generally devoted to knowing and proclaiming truth (as they see it), and this is commendable; however, their approach often restricts their fellowship with other believers.

If I take a *free-minded approach*, I will allow myself to hear and accept anything that attracts me. I will love teaching of any kind but admit that everybody has a right to his own opinion. My doctrine may change weekly, depending upon the last sermon I heard or the latest book I read.

I remember one lady who was always reading the latest popular religious books and devoting herself to their views. One "Christian scholar" she read stated that God uses the stars to make His will known to us. So she became a star-watcher and followed her horoscope for several weeks. Then someone at her church pointed out the biblical passages which condemn astrology, whereupon she deserted her horoscopes and began a new study in communicating with the dead!

While this lady is an extreme example, she serves as a reminder that our faith must be rooted in God's revelation. If our faith has no anchor, we will find ourselves being "carried about by every wind of doctrine" (Eph. 4:14).

Without apology, I believe that Christians should adopt a *tough-minded* approach to their faith. Like narrow-minded believers, tough-minded Christians are devoted to knowing and defending the truth; like the free-minded, they allow themselves to read and learn from many sources. However, they do not turn people away because they disagree; neither do they believe everything they hear.

Tough-minded Christians know what they believe and why. They also know what others believe and why they believe differently. They follow Jesus' example of discussing matters of faith with those who disagree and knowing the difference between essential truth and areas of acceptable variance (Luke 18:18-30; John 4:7-26).

They love to hear all sides of an issue and weigh the evidence by the truth of the Scripture. Their goal is truth; their authority is the Word of God.

Most important, what they believe is not just head knowledge—it is a part of their lives. Their faith affects their behavior because they are convinced of the truth of what they believe. Their faith gives them discernment in applying biblical truth to the world around them. Furthermore, a tough-minded approach allows Christians to respond correctly to those who disagree.

What are the biblical guidelines for responding to opposition? As we mentioned earlier, Christians will find their beliefs challenged on two fronts. Opposition will come from non-Christians who have adopted beliefs that are contrary to what God has revealed. Opposition will also come from fellow Christians who disagree over certain views of Scripture or the practical application of the Scriptures. Let's look at each of these areas separately.

Opposition from the Outside

Janush was a university student in Czechoslovakia. Christians like Janush endured a great deal of ridicule from professors and administrators.

"They always say that God doesn't exist and that Jesus is a myth," he told me. "One professor calls me a fool for believing the Bible."

I tried to be sympathetic. "That's terrible, Janush. How can you put up with that?"

He looked puzzled. "But, Bill," he replied, "they don't know God. They are supposed to treat us like that."

Janush reflected the attitude described by the Apostle Paul: "All who desire to live godly in Christ Jesus will be persecuted" (2 Tim. 3:12). For Janush, opposition from non-Christians was part of being a child of God. He accepted it—and expected it.

Our situation is somewhat different. Whatever opposition we face as Christians is usually at a personal and emotional level.

The fact that non-Christians disagree with us is nothing new. Their disagreements are validated in their minds by the open hypocrisy of many Christians. Those outside of Christianity do not have to look too long to find bad examples of the "Christian faith" in action—the myriad of televangelists who exploit their listeners, the local pastor who is known for his lack of integrity, the Christian businessman who is more concerned about making money than caring for other people. Unfortunately, the examples are endless.

In light of (and in spite of) the misuse of Christian truth, many need to hear a clear presentation of what Christians believe. The tough-minded Christian will initiate opportunities to interact with non-Christians about the faith.

In discussing God's truth with those outside of Christianity, two facts must be kept in mind. First, recognize that spiritual truths are spiritually discerned. Minds that are set only on the things of this world will never understand many of the truths of God. "But a natural man does not accept the things of the Spirit of God; for they are foolishness to him, because they are spiritually appraised" (1 Cor. 2:14).

Second, recognize that Satan is actively blinding the minds of men that they might not accept the truth of God (2 Cor. 4:4). Jesus refers to one who hears the message of God and does not understand it and then has it snatched away by the "evil one" (Matt. 13:19).

Knowledge, Sensitivity, and Godliness

Every Christian is called upon to defend the truth (1 Peter 3:15). Three characteristics should exemplify our approach toward those outside the faith: knowledge, sensitivity, and godliness.

Knowledge. We owe it to others not only to know what *we* believe but also what *they* believe. For too long Christians have stuck their heads in the sand and refused to learn from those outside the faith. The Christians have nothing to fear from a study of worldviews and beliefs different from their own. As long as such a study is accompanied by a healthy and growing knowledge of the Word of God, it only helps to strengthen one's faith.

In my own life, studying the writings of the great skeptics, like Bertrand Russell, T.H. Huxley, Friedrich Nietzche, and others helped me grow in my faith. Try reading an issue of *The American Atheist* and other ramblings by Madalyn Murray O'Hair and her cohorts. It might anger you, but you will probably come away thinking, *Is this the best they can do in arguing against Christianity?*

Sensitivity. Paul wrote, "Conduct yourselves with wisdom toward outsiders, making the most of the opportunity. Let your speech be with grace, seasoned, as it were, with salt, so that you may know how you should respond to each person" (Col. 4:5-6). Paul is speaking here of sensitivity to others as persons. This means we are to be responsive, caring, and willing to listen.

We must ask, What do they believe? Do they have good reasons? Do we genuinely understand what they believe? Are we ready with an answer for the hope that is within us? (1 Peter 3:15)

It is always helpful to know a few good books to share with someone who is interested. This is one of the reasons I have included a Further Reading section at the end of each chapter. Let non-Christians read and learn for themselves.

Many people reject God because of a past hurt. Discussing the evidence for God's existence or the proof for the Trinity could be self-defeating. Rejecting God may be a smoke screen to cover bitterness or anger. Here, sensitivity will allow you to be accepting and loving. Your concern may undo years of internal hatred.

Godliness. Our behavior is to be "excellent" among unbelievers. They are to have no reason to question our lifestyles or motives (1 Peter 2:12). We must not be like those who "profess to know God, but by their deeds they deny Him, being detestable and disobedient, and worthless for any good deed" (Titus 1:16). Our lives are to be walking advertisements for the truth as God has revealed it.

THE DISAGREEABLE BRETHREN

Christians disagree. This is no big secret to Christians or non-Christians. The story of John Wesley and George Whitefield which opened this chapter is a strong reminder that Christians are ONE and belong to the same family. Just as brothers and sisters within a normal household have different views on life, the family of God has a wide range of "sibling rivalries." I am not advocating that anything a Christian believes should be accepted—quite the contrary. My focus in this last section is on the attitude which should prevail as all believers honestly and openly seek to know and apply God's truth.

Timothy, Paul's protégé, faced a number of challenges to his faith. The apostle gave him some guidelines in handling the disagreements which arose among the believers. Note how applicable these are for us today. "But refuse foolish and ignorant speculations, knowing that they produce quarrels. And the Lord's bond servant must not be quarrelsome, but be kind to all, able to teach, patient when wronged, with gentleness correcting those who are in opposition, if perhaps God may grant them repentance leading to the knowledge of the truth" (2 Tim. 2:23-25).

A Godly Approach. Paul tells Timothy to "refuse foolish and ignorant speculations" (2:23). "Ignorant speculations" refers to debates and arguments which are based on little actual knowledge of the matter being argued. The tough-minded Christian will be confronted with many opportunities to argue, but he must know the difference between honest discussion and foolish arguments. Nothing positive is accomplished by Christians sharing their ignorance about an issue. It is not worth the time or effort to argue with individuals who have already made up their minds on a subject and are only talking to defend their position.

Indeed, there are times when we must "contend earnestly for the faith" (Jude 3), but most of the arguing among Christians hardly reaches such an important level.

The tough-minded Christian should help create an atmosphere of open discussion where believers can search the Scriptures together. The goal is not to win arguments but to discover truth.

A Godly Attitude. When Christians disagree over points of doctrine or practice, the most important aspect of the conflict is the attitude demonstrated. Paul writes, "Let no unwholesome word proceed from your mouth, *but only such a word as is good for edification according to the need of the moment,* that it may give grace to those who hear" (Eph. 4:29, emphasis added).

Note the adjectives used in the 2 Timothy passage to describe our attitude: kind, gentle, patient. The overall effect is a humble disposition of the "Lord's bond servant" toward all who disagree. God has saved us to be servants. We "must not be quarrelsome." Even when we are spoken against unjustly, we must not be resentful or bitter. Knowledge of the truth brings about a peace and contentment that does not need to be fed by winning arguments.

As a result of knowing God's truth, tough-minded Christians will be patient and kind in the face of opposition. They will set their hearts "to malign no one, to be uncontentious, gentle, showing every consideration for all men" (Titus 3:2).

A Godly Aim. Paul encourages Timothy (and us) to aim at "correcting those who are in opposition" (2 Tim. 2:25). Paul explains that those who are in error must be corrected. This implies that we have the knowledge to correct them, or, as Paul says, we are "able to teach" (2 Tim. 2:24). When we are confronted with this kind of situation, we must know not only the truth but also the differing views.

Doctrinal errors among Christians are sometimes the result of selfishness and sin rather than intellectual doubt. Paul notes that correction may lead to "repentance" which then leads to the "knowledge of the truth" (2 Tim. 2:25).

A heart of humility eagerly responds to the truth of God. Those who are prideful in what they consider to be their knowledge of the truth are usually the most unteachable. They are not open to any possible alteration of their "truth."

Peaceful Dialogue

When believers discuss their disagreements, a few guidelines would be helpful. First, make certain that everyone understands the subject being discussed. Aristotle wisely stated, "How many a dispute could have been deflated into a single paragraph if the disputants had dared to define their terms."[1] If the subject is inerrancy, the baptism of the

Holy Spirit, or any other hot topic of argument, everyone involved owes it to the others to make certain they are all discussing the same thing.

Second, try to focus on areas of agreement before tackling the controversial topics. Often we forget 99 percent of common ground at the expense of 1 percent of disputed territory.

Third, recognize that the most important questions about how Christianity affects life are being asked by those *outside* of Christianity. Are we focusing too much energy on fighting among ourselves? Are there bigger questions we must answer?

Finally, humility and love must be the pervasive attitude among God's children. We must be open and teachable. What can I learn from my brother with whom I disagree? If I answer "nothing," then I must take an attitude check and examine my own motives.

God's family desperately needs more open dialogue. Such discussion can help believers grow in their knowledge and understanding of the truth. There are times, however, when we must agree to disagree and link arms to get about doing what God has called us to do.

So What?

I enjoy teaching, but I have learned that teaching is more than merely spewing out facts to be memorized until the exam is over. I encourage my students to ask two questions about everything we learn: *Why?* and *So what?* To ask *Why?* is to go beyond the mere facts themselves and get at a greater cause or reason. To ask *So what?* is to question the importance of these facts and how they fit in with everything else we are learning.

One of the purposes of this book is to begin answering the question *Why?* As Christians we need to know what we believe and why, but such knowledge must be gained in the context of a world that disagrees, sometimes violently, with our conclusions.

Knowledge alone is not the final goal. People who are considered knowledgeable today are often those who have mastered great amounts of trivia. Einstein once said, "Imagination is more important than knowledge." His point was that using our minds is more important than filling our minds. Facts are important, but they are only a means to an end. We must seek more than knowing; we must seek understanding.

The Bible does not stop with the command "Know the truth" but adds "Obey the truth." This is one way to answer the question *So what?* Truth demands not only acceptance but also obedience. If all of the truths we have discussed in this book are indeed true, we cannot merely reply, "Well, I know all this," and then be off on our way. The truth is gripping and demanding.

For instance, if I acknowledge that a personal God does exist, the next logical step is to commit myself to a life of dependence on Him. I may try to ignore His presence, but I cannot escape Him. He is there in my most embarrassing moments and my moments of grossest sin. Even my thoughts do not evade His intimate knowledge of me.

The way I treat another person reflects what I believe about his Creator. Paying my income tax honestly demonstrates that I know integrity before God is more important than a few extra dollars. The quantity and intensity of my prayer life shows how much I rely on God's involvement in my life.

Our words should so clearly present God's truth, and our lives should so clearly demonstrate its effectiveness that there are none who could accuse us of hypocrisy. Let them deny the truth of God, but let it not be because we have misrepresented Him by our words or our lives.

A Faith that Won't Break

The story of Daniel and his three friends (Daniel 1–6) has often served as an encouragement for God's people to maintain their commitment to the Lord in the face of strong adversity. What we see in them is a tough-minded approach to their faith in the midst of a hostile society. Let's look at how their lives reflected the essential characteristics we have discussed.

Knowledge. Notice that "God gave them knowledge and intelligence in every branch of literature and wisdom" (Dan. 1:17). They not only knew what the Scriptures taught, but they also knew what other writings taught. They could read and understand pagan literature without believing it. They knew where truths intersected and where error began. This knowledge did not weaken their faith but rather gave their faith a resiliency that stood up against the threat of Nebuchadnezzar's fiery furnace (Dan. 3:15-18) and the lion's den of Darius (Dan. 6:4-24).

Sensitivity. Daniel, Shadrach, Meshach, and Abed-nego conducted themselves "with wisdom toward outsiders" (Col. 4:5). They addressed their superiors with respect (Dan. 1:12) and obeyed authority as long as it did not conflict with God's statutes. When their faith collided with the pagan system, they did not antagonize the unbelievers but sought a resolution agreeable to all (Dan. 1:8-16); however, when their faith was tested to the limit, they never compromised in the name of peace (Dan. 3:16-18; 6:1-28).

Godliness. Daniel and his friends were characterized by a desire to obey God (Dan. 1:8; 6:10-11, 20). Their lives were marked by such integrity that even their enemies could not find anything to criticize (Dan. 6:4-5).

Furthermore, they held a view of God that acknowledged His supremacy in human affairs (Dan. 2:19-23; 27-28). God was not their servant, and they knew that their allegiance to Him gave no guarantee of an easy life. They acknowledged that God very well could deliver them from execution but, then again, He might not (Dan. 3:17-18). Their concern was to obey God regardless of the consequences.

For these men, their faith made sense in an age of unbelief. Fully convinced of the truth, they aggressively lived out what they believed. A blatantly pagan culture and life-threatening decisions served to give them a deeper understanding of their own faith and a greater commitment to live by it.

May God so motivate us to believe and to live.

Discussion Questions

1. How would you characterize a "narrow-minded" and an "free-minded" Christian? What are some practical examples of how these kinds of believers live their "faith?"

2. Describe the "tough-minded" Christian. How will tough-minded Christians be involved in their churches and communities?

3. If it is possible for the narrow-minded and the tough-minded Christian to believe the same, then why are they so different? How would you characterize yourself?

4. Should Christians discuss areas of disagreement? What attitudes should prevail? What insights does 2 Timothy 2:23-25 give?

5. How are Christians to dialogue with non-Christians about the faith? Can you think of some creative ways to encourage discussion with non-Christians personally or through your church?

6. *Why?* and *So what?* are important questions Christians must ask. Explain.

Further Reading

Norman Anderson, ed., *The World's Religions*, rev. ed. (Grand Rapids: William B. Eerdmans, 1977).

William A. Dyrness, *Christian Apologetics in a World Community* (Downers Grove, Ill.: InterVarsity Press, 1983).

Horace L. Fenton, *When Christians Clash* (Downers Grove, Ill.: InterVarsity Press, 1987).

James W. Sire, *The Universe Next Door* (Downers Grove, Ill.: InterVarsity Press, 1976).

NOTES

Chapter One

[1]Stephen Zweig, *The Living Thoughts of Tolstoy* (Philadelphia: David McKay, 1939), p. 4.

[2]Blaise Pascal, *Pensées*, English edition (New York: E.P. Dutton & Co., Inc., 1958), p. 79 (Pensée #280).

[3]These three levels of commitment are adapted from the three levels of valuing described in *Taxonomy of Educational Objectives Handbook 2: Affective Domain* (New York: David McKay, 1964) by D.R. Krathwohl, B.S. Bloom, and B.B. Masia.

Chapter Two

[1]See "Quest for the Most Distant," *Astronomy* (June 1988), pp. 20–27.

[2]This anecdote is recorded in many places. See Robert Hendricksen, *The Literary Life and Other Curiosities* (New York: Viking, 1981).

[3]Bill Durbin, "A Scientist Caught Between Two Faiths," *Christianity Today* (August 6, 1982), p. 15.

[4]Ibid.

[5]Pascal, p. 77 (Pensée #265).

[6]Albert Einstein, *The World As I See It.* Quoted in *The Great Thoughts*, compiled by George Seldes (New York: Ballantine Books, 1985), p. 119.

[7]Tim Stafford, "Cease-Fire in the Laboratory," *Christianity Today* (April 3, 1987), p. 18.

Chapter Three

[1]Eric Temple Bell, *Men of Mathematics* (New York: Simon and Schuster, 1937), p. 181.

[2]Shirley MacLaine, *It's All in the Playing* (New York: Bantam Books, 1987), p. 174.

[3]Kathleen Hughes, "Enlightenment Is Fine, but Now a New Car Will Do," *Wall Street Journal* (May 9, 1986), pp. 1, 16.

[4]André Gide, *Les Nouvelles Nourritures*. Quoted in *The Great Thoughts*, compiled by George Seldes (New York: Ballantine Books, 1985), p. 160.

[5]Kingsley Davis, *Human Society* (New York: Macmillan Company, 1949), p. 544.

[6]The Society of Evangelical Agnostics (SEA), Box 515, Auberry, California 93602. Their motto: "Promoting the principles of agnosticism in all aspects of life."

[7]Stephen Hawking, "The Creation of the Universe," *Nova* special broadcast by Public Broadcasting System, 1985.

[8]C.S. Lewis, *Mere Christianity*, reprint ed. (Westwood,

N.J.: Barbour and Company, 1952), p. 36.

Chapter Four

[1]David Barrett, ed. *World Christian Encyclopedia: A Comparative Study of Churches and Religions in the Modern World, A.D. 1900 to 2000* (New York: Oxford University Press, 1982), pp. 1–21.

[2]Jeff Frankel, "Champions Without Christ," *American Atheist*, (1983/1984), p. 30.

[3]William Paley, *Natural Theology* (London: J. Faulder, 1805), pp. 1–8.

[4]Bertrand Russell, *Why I Am Not a Christian* (New York: Simon and Schuster, 1957), pp. 3–10.

[5]Clifton Fadiman, gen. ed., *The Little, Brown Book of Anecdotes* (Boston: Little, Brown and Company, 1985), p. 336.

[6]Laurence J. Peter, *Peter's Quotations: Ideas for Our Time* (New York: Bantam Books, 1979), p. 124.

[7]Dorothy L. Sayers, *The Mind of the Maker* (Westport, Conn.: Greenwood Press, 1941), pp. 21–31.

Chapter Five

[1]W. Davenport Adams, *Treasury of Modern Anecdote* (London: Thomas D. Morison, 1886), p. 192.

[2]Reported in *Newport (Virginia) News Times-Herald* (March 21, 1983). Quoted in *American Atheist* (1983/1984), p. 5.

[3]Michael Green, *The Second Epistle of Peter and the Epistle of Jude*, Tyndale New Testament Commentaries (Grand Rapids: Wm. B. Eerdmans, 1968), p. 91.

[4]Robert Lightner, *The Saviour and the Scriptures* (Philadelphia: Presbyterian and Reformed Publishers, 1966), p. 285.

[5]John Wenham, *Christ and the Bible* (Downers Grove, Ill.: InterVarsity Press, 1972), p. 13.

[6]For a good description of the Catholic view of the canon, see *The Jerome Bible Commentary*, 2 vols. (Englewood Cliffs, N.J.: Prentice-Hall, Inc., 1968), edited by Raymond E. Brown, Joseph A. Fitzmer, and Roland E. Murphy, 1:515–534. Also see the *New Catholic Encyclopedia* (New York: McGraw-Hill Book Co., 1967), "Bible, III (Canon)," 2:387–391.

[7]Athanasius, *Letters*, no. 39 (Easter sermon, A.D. 367). This discussion is not intended to ignore the complex process of canonization. The details can be found in the Catholic sources cited above as well as in a good Bible dictionary or encyclopedia. Particularly helpful is Roger Beckwith's *The Old Testament Canon of the New Testament Church and its Background in Early Judaism* (Grand Rapids: Wm. B. Erdmans, 1986); and Andrew Walls' "The Canon of the New Testament" in *The Expositor's Bible Commentary*, 12 vols., Frank Gaebelein, gen. ed. (Grand Rapids: Zondervan Publishing House, 1979), 1:631–643.

[8]Donald Bloesch, *Essentials of Evangelical Theology*, 2 vols. (San Francisco: Harper and Row, 1978), 1:63.

[9]Charles W. Keysor, *Our Methodist Heritage* (Elgin, Ill.: David C. Cook Publishing Co., 1973), p. 51.

Chapter Six

[1]Deane William Ferm, "Honest to Jesus," *The Christian Century* (March 22, 1972), pp. 332–335.

[2]Klaas Runia, "A 'New' Christology Challenges the Church," *Christianity Today* (January 4, 1974), pp. 5–6.

[3]John A.T. Robinson, *The Human Face of God* (London: SCM Press, 1973), pp. 207–208.

[4]C.S. Lewis, *Mere Christianity*, reprint ed. (Westwood, N.J.: Barbour and Company, 1952), pp. 45ff.

Chapter Seven

[1]J.B. Phillips, *Plain Christianity and Other Broadcast Talks* (New York: Macmillan Publishing Company, Inc., 1956), p. 104.

Chapter Eight

[1]"The Scripture, Reason, and the Trinity," *Watchtower* (January 1, 1953), p. 22.

[2]Ahmed Deedat, *Al-Qur'an: The Ultimate Miracle* (Istanbul: Inkilab, n.d.), pp. 77–78.

[3]J. Kenneth Grider, "The Holy Trinity," *Basic Christian Doctrines*, ed. by Carl F.H. Henry, reprint ed. (Grand Rapids: Baker Book House, 1971), p. 36.

[4]Nick Herbert, *Quantum Reality: Beyond the New Physics* (Garden City, N.Y.: Anchor/Doubleday, 1985), p. xiii.

[5]C.S. Lewis, *Mere Christianity*, reprint ed. (Westwood, N.J.: Barbour and Company, 1952), pp. 138–139.

[6]For a fuller discussion, see Bruce Demarest's and Gordon Lewis' *Integrative Theology* (Grand Rapids: Zondervan Publishing House, 1987), 1:249–289.

[7]John H. Leith, ed., *Creeds of the Church*, 3rd ed. (Atlanta: John Knox Press, 1982), pp. 21–22.

[8]The full creed is an exposition of the Christian belief in the Trinity. See A.A. Hodge's *Outlines of Theology* (Grand Rapids: Zondervan Publishing Company, 1972), pp. 117–118.

Chapter Nine

[1]This statement sums up Plato's understanding of the ethics of Socrates. See, for example, Plato's "Protagoras," *The Dialogues of Plato*.

[2]James Hastings, ed., *Encyclopedia of Religion and Ethics*, 13 vols. (New York: Charles Scribner's Sons, n.d.), "Salvation," 11:109–151.

[3]Harold Titus, Marilyn S. Smith and Richard T. Nolan, *Living Issues in Philosophy*, 8th ed. (Belmont, Calif.: Wadsworth Publishing Co., 1986), pp. 488–491.

[4]Ibid.

[5]Thomas Aquinas, *Summa Theologica*, part one, question one, article one.

Chapter Ten

[1]Edgar C. Whisenant, *On Borrowed Time* and *88 Reasons Why the Rapture Could Be in 1988* (Nashville: World Bible Society, 1988).

[2]J.B. Phillips, *The Newborn Christian* (New York: Macmillan Publishing Co., Inc., 1978), p. 216.

[3]An interesting and emotional discussion of the New Age understanding of the Second Coming is found in *The Hidden Dangers of the Rainbow* by Constance Cumbey (Shreveport, La.: Huntington House, 1983). Among the best treatments of New Age themes is *Unmasking the New Age* by Douglas Groothuis (Downers Grove, Ill.: InterVarsity Press, 1986).

[4]Charles H. Dodd, *The Apostolic Preaching and Its Development* (Chicago: Willett and Clark, 1937), pp. 79–96.

[5]Anthony A. Hoekema, *The Bible and the Future* (Grand Rapids: Wm. B. Eerdmans, 1979), p. 173–174.

[6] See John J. Davis' *Christ's Victorious Kingdom* (Grand Rapids: Baker Book House, 1987); also see Loraine Boettner's *The Millennium* (Philadelphia Presbyterian and Reformed, 1957).

[7]See John F. Walvoord's, *The Millennial Kingdom* (Findlay, Ohio: Dunlon, 1959); also see George E. Ladd's *The Blessed Hope* (Grand Rapids: Wm. B. Eerdmans, 1952).

Chapter Eleven

[1]Gallup Organization (Princeton, N.J.). Quoted in *The Harper's Index Book* (New York: Henry Holt and Co., 1987), p. 14.

[2]Edward Fudge, "The Final End of the Wicked," *Journal of the Evangelical Theological Society* 27:3 (September 1984), pp. 333–334.

[3]Merrill Holste, "Betting on a Hereafter," *The American Atheist* (1983/1984), p. 25.

[4]Pauline Frederick, *Ten First Ladies of the World* (New York: Meredith, 1967), p. 6.

Chapter Twelve

[1]Laurence J. Peter, *Peter's Quotations: Ideas for Our Time* (New York: Bantam Books, 1979), p. 24.